Staff Welfare Practices
in the Public Schools

THE LIBRARY OF EDUCATION

A Project of The Center for Applied Research in Education, Inc.

G. R. Gottschalk, Director

Categories of Coverage

I	II	III
Curriculum and Teaching	Administration, Organization, and Finance	Psychology

IV	V	VI
History, Philosophy, and Social Foundations	Professional Skills	Educational Institutions

Staff Welfare Practices
in the Public Schools

LESLIE W. *athrow* KINDRED, *1905-*

Professor of Educational Administration
Temple University

PRINCE B. WOODARD

Professor of Educational Administration
Temple University

1963
The Center for Applied Research in Education, Inc.
Washington, D.C.

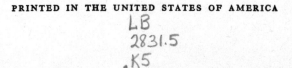

LB
2831.5
.K5

Foreword

This book deals with staff welfare practices in the public schools. The term "welfare" is given a new connotation, embracing as it does the entire realm of psychological, physical, and social well-being as well as material. The treatment of welfare is comprehensive and forward-looking, and it includes the shared thinking of many school superintendents and boards of education.

The importance of the field of personnel administration and the timeliness of the material presented by the authors make this book an attractive and valuable contribution to the literature of school administration.

A major part of the book is devoted to an analysis of personnel policies of a wide sample of school systems in this country. Attention is given to such topics as health and recreation, working conditions and environment, leaves of absence, insurance, legal protection, and other benefits, and how their relationship to staff welfare influences the efficiency and effectiveness of instruction. In addition, many possibilities for fringe benefits are mentioned with reference to class size, time schedules, supplies, and equipment. The problems of teachers concerning housing, standards of community conduct, and other matters of everyday life are treated in a sympathetic and professional manner.

Boards of education and superintendents will find this book most helpful in their search for solutions to staff welfare problems. It should also be stimulating and challenging to teachers, both as individuals and as members of teachers' organizations. A further use can be made of the book in helping to convince the people of the community of their responsibility for improving the working conditions and general welfare of teachers and that there are several means available to them for accomplishing these purposes.

v

No doubt the book contains more ideas and suggestions than any one school system can adopt. In this respect, however, it supplies a ready source of reference and a guide for the development of a reasonable and sound program in personnel administration that is aimed at improving staff welfare.

JOHN B. GEISSINGER
Superintendent of Schools
Tenafly, New Jersey

Contents

CHAPTER I

Introduction

Personnel administration may be defined as that aspect of management which is concerned with the employment, in-service development, utilization, and welfare of the men and women who comprise the operational staff of an organization or an institution.[1] As applied to the administration of public school systems, the purpose of these four functions is to achieve the educational objectives of the state and the local school district. Each requires special treatment in any well-conceived personnel program if established goals are to be reached or approximated satisfactorily.

Of these functions, perhaps the least amount of attention has been given to welfare—especially as it relates to professional staff members. This becomes evident when the personnel policies and practices in a number of school systems are examined.[2] Not only do the systems differ in the treatment of welfare problems but also in the scope of the problems treated. Collectively, however, these policies and practices represent an overview of what is being done to meet welfare needs of staff members, and suggest what could be done to round out welfare programs in local districts.

Before discussing the nature and scope of welfare provisions, it would seem advisable to look at the meaning of welfare and to examine the purposes and importance of this function in the personnel program.

The Meaning of Staff Welfare

The professional staff worker, like any human being, has an interest in his own happiness and prosperity. This interest arises out of deep-seated needs and desires, which, though complex and inter-

---

[1] Based on a statement by Michael J. Jucius, *Personnel Management,* rev. ed. (Chicago: Richard D. Irwin, Inc., 1951), pp. 18–20.
[2] The sample included about 300 school systems located in all states except Alaska and Hawaii.

related, are identifiable. Those which appear to have a strong influence on the well-being of the individual may be classified as health, psychological, social, and economic. They constitute a framework within which the meaning of welfare is found.

Health needs. The degree to which health needs, both physical and mental, are satisfied has an important bearing on human behavior. If they are satisfied reasonably well, it generally follows that the individual is able to take part in vocational and avocational activities without a serious loss of energy or without costly interruptions due to physical discomfort or pain. Moreover, the reasonable satisfaction of these needs assists in promoting a wholesome outlook on life and the acceptance of reality. Most individuals who enjoy fairly good health are also more apt to get along with other people and to engage in socially acceptable behavior.

The desire for good health is tied to a persistent and powerful need for security. Without good health, security is undermined, for example, by prospects of high medical costs, loss of employment, and depletion of family savings. For these reasons, it is understandable that teachers have shown serious concern about exposure to children with diseases, heavy work loads, dangerous and unhealthful conditions of work, the use of medical facilities, provisions for substitute service, and allowance for sick-leave with salary. Their security and their families' security depends in no small measure upon how their health needs are met in employment.

Psychological needs. There is a psychological side to welfare that is reflected in the way teachers view their employment. They may think of themselves as being well-off or of working in an unfavorable situation, depending (1) upon how certain needs are met and (2) upon how they compare in this respect with teachers in other school systems. As to the first point, they want to feel that the administrator has

> ... confidence in them as members of a team; they want to have a share in planning the program; they want to be given full measures of responsibility for its successful operation; they want their contributions recognized; they want to feel that they are growing from day to day and week to week and year to year; they want to feel happy and secure in their positions.[3]

---

[3] *Staff Relations in School Administration,* 33rd Yearbook, American Association of School Administrators (Washington, D.C.: The Association, 1955), p. 83.

There are other needs and desires as well which combine in subtle ways to influence attitudes and convictions of teachers about their work.

As to the second point, teachers translate their employment reactions in comparative terms. For example, they may consider their teaching assignments and non-teaching duties as fair until a policy of "extra pay for extra work" is adopted in a neighboring system. When this happens, their own loads may seem heavy and unjust without extra compensation for time spent beyond the normal working day. Similarly, they may regard the local salary schedule, sick-leave plan, or health protection policy as satisfactory until these are compared with better ones in other school districts. Dissatisfactions arising out of comparisons may be minor, however, if differences are limited to a few items affecting personal welfare and if the differences are not too significant; or they may be minor if benefits on other items are outstanding and yield high satisfaction.

Social needs. A third aspect of welfare includes the social needs of staff personnel—the administrators, supervisors, teachers, and special service workers who are professionally trained. They wish to occupy a position in the community socially equal to that of most citizens, and to have the community accept them as first-rate members. They want the right to a private existence, to be accepted as normal human beings, to feel a sense of personal worth and dignity, and to exercise freedom of choice. They also desire to secure increased public recognition of the teaching profession and especially to have the personal and social value of its services acknowledged and compared with those of the more traditional professions. They believe that increased public recognition would advance their social position in the community.

Social needs are difficult to satisfy in districts where teachers and their colleagues are treated as second-class citizens. Under constant scrutiny, they are denied the full rights and privileges enjoyed by other citizens in such matters as housing, recreation, and social activities. Any deviations made from prevailing customs and traditions are openly criticized and even the "minor vices which characterize so much contemporary social life" are prohibited.[4] The fact that they are expected to take on outside responsibilities (such as

[4] Myron Lieberman, *Education as a Profession* (Englewood Cliffs, N.J.: Prentice-Hall, Inc., 1956), p. 474.

directing youth groups, teaching Sunday school, or soliciting funds for charitable enterprises) often induces a sense of frustration and discouragement.

Economic needs.   Aside from the many personal and social rewards of teaching and its allied activities, members of the profession have to meet the economic realities of life. They must be paid enough for their services to maintain a reasonable standard of living and to protect themselves and their families against the financial consequences of illness, old age, and death. Since teaching affords few opportunities to acquire wealth, the satisfaction of economic needs depends almost entirely upon fixed income. It is not surprising, therefore, that teachers strive constantly to maintain and improve salary levels.

When salary levels are high enough to satisfy fairly well the economic demands of life and to permit the building of financial security against the future, teachers have a more wholesome outlook regarding their welfare and their social position in the community. But when salary levels are initially rather poor and fail to keep pace with the cost of living, their welfare is placed in jeopardy and they develop strong feelings of personal and social insecurity.

Importance of Staff Welfare

Although little research has been done in the public schools to determine the relationship between provisions for welfare and staff effectiveness, the observations and practical experience of administrators furnish a number of generalizations which appear to have validity. The generalization is made that if the board of education and the head of the school system show a constructive interest in the welfare of the personnel, they will receive more cooperation and better performance from teachers and professional workers. A similar conclusion was drawn by Likert from research conducted in industry. He states that "when he [the worker] feels that his boss is genuinely interested in him, his problems, his future, and his well-being, he is more likely to be a higher producer."[5]

Some other pertinent generalizations are: Applicants for teaching positions are recruited more easily in systems that have

---

[5] Rensis Likert, "Motivation: The Core of Management," *Personnel Series, Number 155* (New York: American Management Association, 1953), p. 5.

adequate welfare policies. Men and women with fine minds and high teaching ability are attracted to such systems. When "conditions of employment and service" are satisfactory, the percentage of turnover drops considerably. Teachers who remain in a system because it provides for their welfare needs usually become active and respected members of the community. Furthermore, these teachers find more enjoyment in their work and get along agreeably with their colleagues. There appears to be a relationship between provisions for welfare and the mental and physical health of teachers as well as their loyalty to the school system.

Perhaps the most important generalization of all is that the quality of instruction received by pupils is better when sound and adequate welfare provisions are legally adopted by the board of education. The reasons behind this statement are summed up partly in the opinion that

> . . . real improvement in the educational program comes through the improvement of classroom teachers. Any practice that contributes to the competency and security of classroom teachers is reflected in better teaching and learning. A sense of personal growth and a feeling of satisfaction derived from one's work are key factors in good morale and self-improvement.[6]

It is self-evident that instructional efficiency cannot be conceived apart from the physical, intellectual, and emotional capabilities of teachers who direct the learning process.

Accepted Purposes

As implied previously, welfare policies in the personnel program are directed toward the attainment of several interrelated purposes. These purposes vary specifically with school systems due to differences in local needs and conditions and in the kinds of concern shown by the board of education for staff welfare. Those most commonly accepted and emphasized in policies today are listed below.

1. To increase staff efficiency in carrying out the philosophy and objectives of the school system.
2. To provide employment conditions which facilitate the performance of duties and responsibilities.

---

[6] *The Superintendent as Instructional Leader,* 35th Yearbook, American Association of School Administrators (Washington, D.C.: The Association, 1957), p. 53.

3. To establish a psychological climate that promotes continuing cooperation on the part of staff personnel.

4. To protect and enhance the mental and physical health of professional workers.

5. To eliminate annoyances and worries which interfere with the efficient performance of services.

6. To create a strong sense of security on the part of professional personnel.

7. To improve the social status of staff members in the community.

8. To bring out each individual's potential for professional growth and development.

9. To develop a fine esprit de corps among staff members of the school system.

10. To promote friendly relationships among all classes of professional workers.

11. To attract high-grade young people into teaching and to hold experienced and capable teachers in service.

12. To increase the amount of satisfaction individual staff members derive from their employment.

Experience seems to indicate that a reasonable attainment of these purposes, or others similar to them, contributes substantially to the happiness of staff members and the quality of instruction conducted by them.

Policy Preparation

Personnel policies are formal plans of action for achieving the immediate and long-range goals of the state and the local school system. Developed and organized around the mutual concerns of the state and district and the men and women who render professional services, they are also legal means for facilitating cooperation and improving efficiency in the performance of the services rendered. Among these policies are a number which pertain to the welfare of staff members. Some are financial in character, such as those relating to salary, insurance, retirement, sick leave, credit unions, and the like, while others are nonfinancial in character, such as those relating to recreation, housing, community status, elimination of pressures, and other environmental conditions.

While there is no assurance that welfare policies in themselves will produce the results that are wanted, there is enough evidence from administrative observations and experiences to support the assumption that such policies stimulate cooperation and increase work efficiency when they are based on the needs and desires of staff members as well as the interests of the institution.

In designing welfare policies, problems are often encountered which demand careful study and treatment. A major problem in this respect is the question of how

> . . . to recognize and provide for the attitudes, feelings, and needs of individuals . . . , and at the same time succeed in welding a school system into a working unit from top to bottom. Actually the two tasks are not opposites; they are complementary—the individual striving for success of the system and the system supporting the desires and freedoms of the individual.[7]

An answer must be found to this basic question, but the answer must be one that keeps both sides in balance.

Prevailing conditions within a school system frequently have an influence on the reactions of staff members to welfare proposals. The ready acceptance of an in-service training program, for example, may be due to a happy state of mind over salary and insurance arrangements rather than to the merits of the program. On the other hand, sound suggestions for increasing staff participation in the administration may be turned down simply because of strong discontent over the persistent negligence of administrators to eliminate or sharply reduce class interruptions for various kinds of drives and athletic contests. The same negative manifestation may be observed in the importance teachers attach to minor physical inconveniences —such as torn window shades or noise from an adjoining playground—when there is discord between the staff and administration.

In developing welfare policies care must be taken to review the dynamics of human behavior and to understand the pressures encountered in daily living. Too often policies are centered around material problems to the exclusion of other factors which have an impact on attitudes, feelings, and work performance. In a given community, for instance, it might be highly important to adopt a policy recognizing the right of every teacher to a private existence and to offer means for helping him become identified with the social

---

[7] *Staff Relations in School Administration, op. cit.,* p. 83.

and cultural life of the community. Teachers usually respond constructively to actions which reveal understanding and concern for human needs and problems and which go further than the economics of everyday living. Certainly more favorable attitudes would be developed if the board of education granted short leaves of absence without loss of salary for attending to family emergencies.

It should be noted likewise that attitudes and actions are sometimes affected more by the way welfare policies are determined than by the benefits provided. Staff members react negatively to decisions made by those in higher authority when their own points of view are not take into consideration or when they are consulted after the decisions are already formulated.

Scope of the Treatment

Virtually every school district in this country has policies of one kind or another for protecting and advancing the welfare of its employees. Some are mandated by statute and carry options permitting the local district to supplement the basic prescriptions of the state. Others represent the products of a sincere and continuing concern by district boards of education to meet the welfare needs of teachers and other professional workers. And still others, though outside the jurisdiction of state and local education authorities, are encouraged and endorsed by local boards and their administrative officers.

In the chapters that follow only passing recognition will be given to state-mandated and locally-adopted policies and provisions for tenure, retirement, salary, and load.[8] The focal point will be instead on various policies and practices followed by local districts, their similarities and differences, and concepts that should be included in provisions for welfare in school personnel programs today.

Plans will also be reviewed for servicing welfare needs through programs that operate without control by the district, but which often receive its endorsement and support.

---

[8] For a more detailed discussion of these topics, see other volumes in the Library of Education series dealing with personnel and administration.

CHAPTER II

Health and Recreation

It is essential for school districts to staff each classroom with a healthy teacher. There are several reasons why teacher health should be given primary concern in personnel policies. Only two, however, need be cited: first, sound health is essential for superior teaching; second, each pupil has a right to a healthful classroom environment. The Report of the Joint Committee of the National Education Association and the American Medical Association on Health Problems in Education stated the importance of teacher health in clear terms:

> For instructional employees health is important for the support it gives to good teaching personality. The effectiveness of the teacher, whose work constantly involves human relations, is a reflection of his own good mental and physical health.[1]

A healthy person is one who is sound of mind and body. Each individual has a personal responsibility for maintaining sound health; it is an obligation he owes to himself and to society. While it can be hoped that every teacher and teacher-applicant will recognize this responsibility and utilize every facility and resource available to maintain good health, those responsible for staffing the schools must not operate on this assumption. Rather, they must require that physical and mental health standards be met for initial and continued employment. This can be accomplished through the formulation of health policies and the establishment of requirements, practices, and services to make this policy operative.

This chapter identifies desirable policy and practices concerning physical health, mental health, and recreational needs of teachers and describes what selected school districts are accomplishing in these areas.

---

[1] Charles C. Wilson, ed., *School Health Services,* a Report of the Joint Committee on Health Problems in Education of the NEA and AMA (Washington, D.C.: National Education Association, 1953), p. 356.

Physical Health

Although it is generally agreed that teachers are as physically healthy as other professional groups, it was estimated that public school teachers in our nation lost at least 1,450,000 days from teaching because of illness in the school year 1954–55.[2] Irrespective of the comparative health status of teachers with other groups, teacher absenteeism for physical illness does reduce the quality of instruction provided to pupils. Still worse is the fact that teachers who remain on the job when ill subject their pupils to an unhealthy environment.

The loss of teachers from the job because of physical infirmities cannot be completely prevented, nor can the possibility of ill teachers remaining on the job be completely eliminated. Both can be substantially reduced by the enactment and application of a physical health policy by each local school district which (1) requires medical evidence of sound physical health for initial employment and continued employment, and (2) provides physical health services to the teaching staff.

Physical examinations. The physical examination is recognized as the best method for determining the status of an individual in relation to established physical criteria. At present 34 states have physical examination requirements for teachers. These states frequently insist that a doctor's certificate attesting to the general good health of the individual or a statement to the effect that the subject is free from certain communicable diseases be included with his application. The result of a chest x-ray and a report on a sight and/or hearing test are other requirements frequently found in these states. Such state requirements should be regarded by the local school district as minimum standards. Each district should establish its own thorough and comprehensive examination requirement for determining the physical health status of its employed teachers and its teacher applicants.

Currently, local school-district physical examination requirements differ widely. A study of personnel practices in urban school districts in 1955–56 revealed that only 42 per cent of the 1973 dis-

---

[2] *The Status of the American Public-School Teacher,* Research Bulletin 35 (Washington, D.C.: Research Division, National Education Association, February, 1957), p. 49.

tricts reporting had a local regulation concerning compulsory health examinations for teachers. Of those districts requiring an examination, 40 per cent had an annual requirement, 24 per cent a biannual requirement, and 36 per cent of the districts stated that their requirement was at intervals longer than two years.[3] Some local school districts, even in states without statewide requirements, do not require health examinations for teachers. Other local districts view their state regulation as adequate and have no supplementary examination requirement. A third group of districts, some in states without requirements and others in states with minimum requirements, have formulated broad policies on teacher health and have established detail regulations concerning physical examinations.

Although local regulations concerning teacher physical examinations may differ, each should include an answer to at least these questions: Who must be examined? When must an examination be given? What should an examination include? Who may administer the examination? How should the results of the examination be processed?

Who must be examined? All personnel employed to teach in the school must meet the health standards established by the school district: thus a physical examination should be required for all such personnel. Included in this classification are the regular full-time teachers, part-time teachers, substitutes, teacher-aides, and all others who are assigned classroom responsibilities with pupils. Unfortunately, many school districts prescribe a physical examination only for regular full-time teachers.

When must the examination be given? The frequency of examinations must vary with circumstances. Both a pre-employment examination as well as an annual examination should be required without exception. The medical profession is vocal in its endorsement of the annual examination for all healthy adults. Acceptance of a lesser requirement for teachers is indefensible, although a 1956 survey indicated that less than twenty per cent of the urban school districts in the nation had a local regulation which required an annual examination of all teachers.[4]

---

[3] *Teacher Personnel Practices, Urban School Districts, 1955–56* (Washington, D.C.: Research Division, National Education Association, Special Memo., June, 1956), p. 32.

[4] *Ibid.*, p. 32.

Some argue that a compulsory physical examination requirement for teachers is not necessary on the grounds that professional educators will obtain their annual examination without coercion. Unfortunately this is not true. There are many teachers who do not accept the value of the annual physical examination and, like many other adults, fail to heed the advice of the medical profession.

In addition to an annual examination, the local regulation should require one whenever a teacher returns to work from a prolonged absence, a leave for personal illness, family illness, and travel-leave, or whenever there is an accumulation of short separate absences for personal illness. In addition, the regulation should require a physical examination of any teacher whenever conditions and circumstances suggest that his physical health is not good.

The following is a sound example of a local school-district regulation prescribing the frequency of the physical examination:

> Before a contract with an applicant appointed for the first time becomes binding, the individual shall have passed an approved thorough physical examination administered by one of the Board of Public Education's medical examiners. . . .
> Yearly physical examinations including urinalysis, chest x-rays and such other special examinations as recommended by the examining physician are required of all employees. These examinations must be given by the medical staff of the Board of Public Education or by specialists recommended by them.[5]

What should the examination include?   In addition to a physical examination, a written report of medical data, medical judgments, and medical recommendations should be provided. Each is important if the examination requirement is to be of maximum value. The medical data should be of sufficient scope to permit an accurate estimate of the current health status of the individual. Of extreme importance are checks for contagious diseases, physical stamina, accurate determination of visual and hearing acuity, and symptoms of poor mental health or nervous and emotional disturbances. The examining physician should be required to give his opinion as to how the individual's health may affect his performance as a teacher. The physician should also be asked to list his recommendations for any additional examinations which seem desirable

---

[5] *Personnel Policies and Procedures, Wilmington Public Schools* (Wilmington, Del.: Board of Education), p. 31.

and to enumerate any adverse influences that teaching might have on the health of the individual.

Who should administer the examination? There are also great differences in the administration of examinations. Some districts require the teacher to pay for the examination but grant free choice in selecting an examining physician. Others assume the cost of the examination and require the teacher to be examined by the school physician or one of several doctors designated by the district. In still other districts the teacher is given the option of a free examination by district medical personnel or the privilege of selecting the physician of his choice and assuming the cost involved. Of the districts reporting in 1955–56, fifty-one per cent paid the expense of the examination, but in forty-nine per cent of the districts the teachers bore the cost.[6]

While there are arguments favoring the free choice of physician by the teacher, the better practice is to require use of the school doctor or other doctors designated by the school district. Should the district grant the teacher freedom to chose his physician, the district should reserve the right to require additional data from the physician or to require a supplementary examination by a school-designated physician whenever this seems necessary. The following excerpts from local school district regulations illustrate the variation found in current practices.

> The Board of Education requires that each member of the school staff shall have a physical examination each school year. . . . There is no cost to the teacher if the examination is given by a school physician, provided that the appointment for the examination is made through the health office and is at the convenience of the physician.[7]
>
> All the employees of the Fargo Board of Education, upon entering the service of the public schools shall be required to submit a statement attesting to their physical fitness and freedom from tuberculosis, such statement to be prepared by a licensed physician. . . . It shall be deemed the responsibility of the individual employee to provide this certificate which shall be done at his expense.[8]
>
> Every employee of the Manhasset Public Schools must have an

---

[6] *Teacher Personnel Practices, Urban School Districts, 1955–56, op. cit.,* p. 32.
[7] *General Regulations Pearl River Public Schools* (Pearl River, New York: Board of Education, 1960–61), p. 2.
[8] *Fargo Board of Education Policies Manual* (Fargo, North Dakota: Board of Education, August 12, 1958), p. 37.

annual medical examination. . . . All personnel who have received tenure will be encouraged to submit complete physical examination reports from their private physicians but may be examined by the school physician if they prefer. All personnel who have received tenure may have laboratory work performed either privately or by a school-designated laboratory. The expenses of examinations performed by the school physician will be paid by the Board of Education. . . . The expenses of initial laboratory and x-ray work each year will be paid by the Board of Education if the work is performed under the direction of the school health department. . . . The Board of Education reserves the right to have the school physician examine any employee in the system at its discretion. . . . All personnel who are not on tenure must have their annual physical examination performed by the school physician and their laboratory and x-ray work performed by a school-designated laboratory. The expense of this work will be paid by the Board of Education.[9]

How should the examination results be processed and maintained? Physical examination findings must be processed and maintained in a confidential manner. Each completed examination report should be submitted directly by the examining party to a school-designated medical officer who should review the information and report his recommendations to the responsible administrator. This medical officer should file and maintain the health records in a confidential manner. Under no circumstances should a nonprofessional staff member see a teacher's file which contains this examination record.

The responsible administrator, upon receipt of the medical officer's report, should notify the teacher of his status and indicate any additional action required. Portions of the Topeka, Kansas, regulation are cited as an excellent illustration of the proper use of the physical examination report:

An examining board of six physicians has been appointed to examine all prospective employees. The names and business addresses of these physicians will be sent to all prospective employees prior to the effective employment date by the Supervisor of Health, Physical Education and Safety. The prospective employee is expected to make an appointment for a physical examination with one of these physicians. This examination must be completed two weeks prior to the effective employment date.

---

[9] *Rule of Manhasset Board of Education* (Manhasset, New York: Board of Education). Approved 7/1/55 and amended.

During the source of the examination, each person is required to sign a statement releasing the evidence of the examination to The Public Schools of Topeka, with the understanding that this information will be treated confidentially. In addition to the physical examination, each person will be required to have a chest x-ray. The cost of this x-ray will be borne by the school district.

Each physician will submit his findings for each person he examines to the Supervisior of Health, Physical Education and Safety on forms provided for that purpose.

The contract with each newly employed person is contingent upon verification of good health as shown by the examination, and the judgment of the examining physician or other competent medical authority, that the applicant is a good employment risk. In the report of this judgment, the physician will be asked to list all of the health deficiencies discovered by the examination that would hinder him from being fully effective in the position for which he was appointed, and that could be corrected.

If a person is judged to be a good employment risk, but has a health deficiency which can and should be corrected in order for him to be fully effective, he will be expected to secure those corrections. In such a case, the person will make an appointment, at his own expense, for a re-examination no later than January 10th next. Unless evidence of removal or normal progress toward removal of health deficiencies is shown, the employee shall not be considered for employment the following year. . . .

Periodic Physical Examination of All School Employees. Each school employee will be required to have a physical examination every three years of service with The Public Schools of Topeka. The examination will be required for continued employment. If the employee chooses to be examined by a member of the Examining Board, appointed by the Board of Education for that purpose, the cost of the examination will be borne by the school district. However, the employee may choose to be examined by his personal or private physician, and in this instance, the employee will bear the cost of the examination. The report of this periodic physical examination shall be made by the examining physician to the Supervisor of Health, Physical Education and Safety on forms provided by the school district, and shall include not only objective evidence, but also a clear value judgment concerning the physical condition of the employee. In reporting his judgment, the physician will be asked to list all of the health deficiencies discovered by the examination that may be hindering him from being fully effective in his position, and stating which of the deficiencies could be corrected.

If an employee is reported to have health difficulties which could and should be corrected in order for him to be fully effective in his position, he will be expected to secure those corrections. In such a case the employee will make an appointment at his expense for a re-examination within a period of six months.[10]

Medical and Nursing Services

By providing the staff with the services of school medical personnel, local school districts have an excellent opportunity to promote staff health and welfare. Unfortunately, few districts include such provisions in their personnel policies.

In contrast, American industry has been expanding medical services for its employees for the past 50 years. Although school districts may not be able to match the comprehensive employee medical services provided by industry, they can frequently make available limited medical services at little cost to the district. The health benefits of these services to the staff can be of special importance and their morale value may more than offset the dollar costs.

Providing teachers with the services of the school doctor for consultations, examinations, and inoculations is a valuable welfare provision. Each year there are teachers who become concerned about their physical health and need medical counsel. The opportunity to consult with the school doctor can be helpful in determining, for example, the wisdom of postponing medical treatment until the next holiday or the end of the school year, or in obtaining an appointment with an appropriate local physician.

The school doctor may also provide teachers with free examinations whenever they are anxious about their health, and also when an examination report is needed for such purposes as insurance, travel, marriage, scholarships, and the like. In addition to blood tests, urinalysis tests, x-rays, visual acuity and auditory tests, the school doctor might provide inoculations and vaccinations against poliomyelitis, influenza, childhood diseases, and other common maladies.

The school nurse can also make a unique and significant contribution to staff health. At present her services are usually limited to the rendering of first aid assistance to those who are hurt or who become ill while at school. This is a beneficial service but a highly restricted one. A more comprehensive service to the staff would

---

[10] *The Topeka Plan of Working Together For Better Public Schools* (Topeka, Kan.: Board of Education, September, 1960), pp. 89–90.

include emergency home or hospital assistance. Some teachers, especially those who have no local relatives and who live alone in rented facilities, would feel more secure in knowing that the school nurse could be called for temporary aid should an emergency develop. This provision may be regarded as a limited counterpart to the company nurse who, in this way, has supplied medical service to her co-workers for years.

In recent times more and more school districts have employed specialists who provide dental inspections and limited dental care for pupils. Some have made this service available—at a saving in both time and cost—to members of the staff.

Only a few school districts have written personnel policies or procedures which offer their staffs all the physical health services described in the preceding paragraphs. The policy statements which follow are cited as characteristic of those found in the few districts currently providing limited medical and nursing services for their staffs.

> Limited medical services of an advisory nature are available to the employees through the health service department. No treatment is available.[11]
>
> Any service that is available to the child is also available to the staff members. This includes eye testing, audiometer testing, etc.[12]
>
> The School Medical Department shall be interested in the health of all employees at all times. They shall administer screening tests, give health guidance and make proper referrals when requested or offer these services when their observations indicate a need to do so.[13]

Other Services

In a few school districts hospital rooms are available on a limited basis to staff personnel. (These rooms have usually been endowed through grants, wills, and money gifts of individuals and lay and professional groups.) Although not financed by the school district, the district is frequently responsible for the administration of the service. The value of these facilities in the staff health program are

---

[11] *Personnel Policies and Procedures, Denver Public Schools* (Denver, Colo.: Board of Education, 1959), p. 20.

[12] Letter from the Superintendent, Township of Union Schools, Union, New Jersey: January 24, 1961.

[13] *Administrative Regulation 06.12, Upper Merion School District* (Upper Merion, Pa.: Board of Education). Mimeographed.

obvious, and local school districts should exert every effort to promote endowments of this nature.

Teachers in the Philadelphia school system have for their use nine endowed hospital rooms located in four major hospitals within the city.[14] Free board and floor nurse service are included with these rooms and, frequently, certain medical and surgical services as well. In addition to hospital rooms, employees of the Philadelphia schools have the benefit of six endowment funds established to help defray hospital expenses. These endowed hospital rooms and services have been provided by the Philadelphia Teachers Association, The Women Teachers Organization, The Public School Council, and by wills of interested individuals. The eligible teacher-patient is entitled to the continuous use of one of these rooms for four weeks, with a time extension at the end of this period if there is no other applicant for the room. Allocation of rooms and the administration of this service are a responsibility of one of the associate superintendents.

The Virginia Education Association Preventorium for Teachers at the University of Virginia Hospital in Charlottesville, Virginia, is a cooperative welfare service which provides teachers with excellent health care at moderate cost. The Preventorium was developed through the cooperative efforts of the University of Virginia Hospital and the Virginia Education Association in 1929 to provide "preventive treatment of teachers to avoid breakdown in service."[15] Operating continuously since that time it has been expanded as a wing of the hospital.

> Now operated by a full time Medical Director, assisted by a secretary, and a nurse's aide, the Preventorium consists of 17 single bed rooms and one double room, a large lounge with television, nurses station, utility room, and kitchen, in addition to the office and examining room—all air conditioned. Valuable aid by the professional staff of the University Hospital is available as needed.[16]

Use of the Preventorium is limited to active members of the Virginia Education Association. Those who wish to join the Pre-

---

[14] *Administrative Bulletin No. 17, School District of Philadelphia* (Philadelphia, Pa.: Board of Education, November 1, 1959), pp. 9–11.

[15] *VEA Preventorium for Teachers* (Richmond, Va.: Virginia Education Association, n.d.).

[16] *Ibid.*

ventorium pay an initial four dollar membership fee and an annual fee of two dollars. Membership in this organization entitles the individual to consultation and treatment by members of the regular staff of the University of Virginia Hospital. Complete hospitalization, including all services and medical and surgical fees, is provided for a maximum per diem cost of nineteen dollars and fifty cents for the exact number of days hospitalized. Membership in the Preventorium in 1959–1960 numbered 9496 and the total number of patients for the same year was 869.[17]

Services and facilities similar to those available to teachers in Philadelphia and Virginia are possible in many school districts. Any district vitally interested in staff health will encourage citizens, community organizations, and professional agencies to provide these types of facilities and services for teachers.

Workmen's Compensation

Teachers in the large majority of school districts have limited physical health protection through the provisions of state workmen's compensation laws. These laws differ among states, but in general they provide reimbursement for medical and hospital costs which result from injuries sustained on the job and for earnings lost because of an injury. Most of these laws have maximums on the length of time for which payments will be made and also on the total amount which may be paid. The monetary and time limits vary not only among states, but also according to the classification of disability. The range in time-coverage is from 60 days to life and in medical-cost-coverage from three hundred dollars to full cost payment irrespective of amount.[18] Benefits are processed and paid by a state agency from a fund established by mandated scheduled contributions paid by employers.

Although each state does provide some coverage for public as well as private employees, it is difficult to define the exact protection these workmen's compensation laws afford teachers. For instance, in some states the law fails to define who may be classified as a

<hr>

[17] *Preventorium Committee Report* (Richmond, Va.: Virginia Education Association, September 17, 1960), p. 2.
[18] *The Teacher and the Law,* Research Monograph 1959-Mc. (Washington, D.C.: Research Division, National Education Association, September, 1959), p. 72.

public employee and thus leaves the question of teacher coverage in doubt. In other states the law limits coverage to employees in hazardous occupations and at the same time fails to specify clearly which occupations are considered hazardous. Finally, some states permit workmen's compensation coverage for public employees to be a matter of local election. According to a 1959 survey, five states required public employee coverage for only hazardous positions, ten states permitted the coverage of public employees to be determined locally, thirty-two states required coverage for all public employees, and three states required coverage except that they did permit the employer with a very small number of employees the option of providing or withholding coverage for his employees.[19]

Local school districts have at least a two-fold responsibility concerning workmen's compensation coverage for their teachers. First, in those states where the law provides permissive but non-mandatory coverage, local districts should act to establish these benefits for their employees. They should also exercise their influence to have vague and unclear laws amended. Second, school districts should inform their employees of the exact protection they have under workmen's compensation. This would help teachers plan for comprehensive insurance protection and would prevent the payment of insurance premiums for unnecessary overlapping coverage. It would also help teachers to compare more accurately their coverage with those provided to employees in other fields. Districts should also acquaint their teachers with exact information on the procedure to be followed in processing workmen's compensation claims. Frequently the law requires a notification of injury or the filing of a claim within certain time limits for maximum benefits to be paid. Informing teachers of these provisions is a valuable personnel administrative practice.

Mental Health

It is an accepted fact that there is a close relationship between physical and mental health. Therefore a policy which promotes sound physical health for teachers will likely contribute to their mental health. This does not mean, however, that further consider-

---

[19] *Ibid.*, pp. 70–71.

ation of teacher mental health is unnecessary. Each aspect of personnel administration has potential mental health implications, and each personnel policy should be viewed in light of its contribution to the emotional balance and psychological adjustment of the staff.

Statistical data on which to formulate judgments concerning the general mental health status of teachers are extremely limited. In 1941, Dr. Emil Altman, who had served as chief medical examiner of the New York City Board of Education for approximately 17 years, estimated that the incidence of mental illness in the teaching profession was probably about the same as that of the general population. He indicated also that the records in the New York Medical Division showed that approximately 12 per cent of the professional staff members in the public school system of New York were mentally unfit to teach.[20] Whether this and other estimates are high or low, the fact remains that whenever a classroom is staffed with a mentally ill or emotionally upset teacher the pupils suffer. Both Lieberman and the Commission on Health in Schools of the American Association of School Administrators have stated the case well.

> The potential harm that an unbalanced teacher can do, plus the fact that teaching appears to involve more strain than most occupations, justifies greater professional concern with the mental health of the profession than has been accorded to it in the past.[21]
>
> Fortunate, indeed, is the pupil whose teacher has a sound body, a keen sense of humor, and a cheerful outlook on the world both inside and outside of school. Since a direct relationship between the attitude of a pupil and the amount he learns has been established, a pupil whose attitude so largely reflects that of his teacher can learn best under a teacher who is physically, mentally, and emotionally strong.[22]

Both teacher education institutions and state boards of education have an obligation to prevent the mentally unfit from entering the teaching profession. The institutions should observe, test, and counsel with students and, in this way, channel those not suited for teaching into other fields. Certification policies should be estab-

---

[20] Emil Altman, "Our Mentally Unbalanced Teachers," *American Mercury*, 52 (April, 1941) 391–401.

[21] Myron Lieberman, *Education As A Profession* (Englewood Cliffs, N.J.: Prentice-Hall, Inc., 1956), p. 238.

[22] *Health in Schools*, 20th Yearbook, American Association of School Administrators (Washington, D.C.: National Education Association, 1951), p. 46.

lished by state boards of education which require that mental health standards be satisfied as a prerequisite for a teaching certificate.

The primary responsibility for securing and maintaining a teaching staff with sound mental health rests with the local school district. To carry out this responsibility the board should enact policies designed for this specific purpose—policies that outline the need for psychological, psychiatric, and other specialized services for the staff and for the development and maintenance of a satisfying working environment for teachers.

Specialized services. The procedure for determining the mental health status of teacher applicants should be stated in the recruitment information of the school district and should be further explained to each individual applicant at the time of initial contact.

The regular full-time school psychologists and the school psychiatrists can make valuable contributions as members of staff screening committees that are created to interview and screen teacher applicants. Involvement of these specialists is one way of obtaining a check on the mental health of the applicant. The American Association for Health, Physical Education, and Recreation in its 1957 Yearbook on teacher health suggests what the administrator might do.

> The need for the administrator to make certain, to the greatest extent possible, that the prospective employee is sound mentally is far more difficult than that of appraising the applicant's physical health. Records or reports of previous difficulties are seldom available. Occasionally the administrator will be able to get some leads from the candidate's associates. Generally, however, he must depend upon his own ability as an observer in an interview situation. Extreme nervousness, narrow interests, lack of friends and social life, a tendency to be moody or depressed, and a lack of openness in conversation may be signals for caution. When there is possibility for doubt, he may wish to arrange a social situation where some of the teachers or others can also have an opportunity to observe the candidate.[23]

More important than the services school mental health specialists render in the screening and selection process of new teachers is the consultation service they can provide to individual staff members.

---

[23] *Fit To Teach.* Yearbook of the American Association for Health, Physical Education, and Recreation (Washington, D.C.: National Education Association, 1957), pp. 107, 113.

The consultative function of these specialists would be to assist teachers in maintaining sound mental health. Except in unusual situations, it should not be their function to treat teachers with substandard mental health. Their services should be classified as preventative, not curative. This distinction must be understood by the total staff if these specialists are to make their maximum contribution. Teachers should be encouraged to seek counsel from the school psychologist or school psychiatrist whenever they have emotional concerns, just as they are invited to seek the advice of the school physician when they are concerned about their physical well-being. Likewise, administrators should make appropriate referrals to these specialists in the same way that they refer teachers to physical health specialists. (The school district should make this service available for all teachers.) Wilson has stated this practice in its proper perspective.

> For an employee to be recommended to consult a psychiatrist or a psychologist is as fitting as to refer him to a heart specialist. In physical disorders and in those involving the mind and the emotions, early recognition is of greatest importance.[24]

Scates has endorsed a specific procedure for providing mental health counsel for teachers.

> A factual understanding of the emotional problems of teachers, with a knowledge of their structure and history, would probably lead to setting up personal growth centers in school systems which would not report names to the administration. Schools generally lag far behind industry in the establishment of personnel services.[25]

Although the need and value of offering specialized mental health services for teachers is clear, it is unusual to find a school district with a written policy providing for psychological, psychiatric, or any type of mental health counseling for teachers; nor is there evidence that these services are made available even on an unofficial basis. This is an unfortunate situation and one deserving attention.

Few districts have even taken the precaution to enact a policy stating that the school district reserves the right to refer teachers for mental health examinations and consultations when conditions war-

---

24 Wilson, *op. cit.*, pp. 361–62.
25 Douglas E. Scates, "The Stresses and Strains of Teaching: Do We Understand Them?," *Journal of Teacher Education*, 2 (December, 1951), 302–305.

rant such action. The adoption of at least this minimum policy should be given high priority by every school district as a means of protecting both teachers and pupils. The Denver school district has stated its policy in a simple yet comprehensive manner:

> When a physical or mental condition seems to be present that interferes with, or is likely to interfere with, the safety or the health of the pupils, the employee himself, or other employees, a special health examination may be required of the employee.[26]

Recreation

The contribution of recreation to the welfare of the individual has been stated and restated since the days of the Greek philosophers. In recent years our society has expressed increasing concern over the recreational needs and activities of both the adult and youth population. An increasing number of recreational services are being offered to the public by federal, state, and local government agencies. A variety of civic, social, and professional organizations are active in promoting recreation with all age groups. Business and industry sponsor recreational opportunities for their employees. All of these groups seek to acquaint individuals with the personal benefits derived from recreation. In addition, they sponsor a variety of recreational opportunities and facilities. The choice of whether or not to participate remains with the individual.

As a major educational agency of society and as an employer of personnel, it is especially appropriate for the local school district to be concerned with the recreation of its employees.

School sponsored recreation. The typical school district makes no more than a token effort to provide recreational opportunities for teachers and has no written policy on this matter. One of the few printed statements available on teacher recreational provisions is found in a recruitment brochure prepared by the Colorado Springs Public Schools.

> *Recreation Program*
> Bowling—All employees have an opportunity to compete in a weekly bowling league.
> Family Fun—The new gymnasiums and swimming pools at the high schools are available for family use.

---

[26] *Personnel Policies and Procedures, Denver Public Schools, op. cit.,* p. 20.

Outdoor Recreation—Golf, tennis, biking, picnics, and other outdoor activities are enjoyed by all.
Cultural Activities—Opportunities are available for concerts,
plays, lectures, and other cultural programs.[27]

While this statement identifies varied recreational activities, only
bowling and the use of the gymnasiums and swimming pools are
listed as school sponsored.

The few activities which are frequently sponsored by districts
include an annual tea, reception, picnic, seasonal party, or dance;
a faculty play or show (this is often used as a money-raising activity
for the school); a faculty or student-faculty athletic contest; and
occasional trips to historical locations, cultural centers, or special
events.

Private business and industry, on the other hand, invest large
sums in leisure-time activities for their employees. A survey of 287
industrial firms of all types and sizes which sampled industry's attitude toward employees' off-duty activities, revealed that 68 per cent
offered an organized program.[28] Activities most often provided were
sports, dances, outings, movies, hobby development clubs, and the
use of libraries. The National Industrial Association estimated that
a group of 25,000 companies spent over one billion dollars providing recreation for employees in 1957.[29] Included were such companies as Abbott Laboratories which hires a professional art
instructor to give courses to employees, Vannegut Hardware Company of Indianapolis with a 40-piece employee concert band, the
Shell Oil Company with its employee-staged Shell Playhouse, the
National Cash Register Company which provides its employees
with a country club including two 18-hole golf courses, and some
1000 companies which support employee recreation by offering
travel clubs, camera clubs, toastmasters clubs, music groups, lecture
series, athletic programs, drama organizations, and others.

Many school districts can provide a variety of recreational opportunities of a physical, social, and cultural nature for teachers and
their families at minimum cost to the district. This is possible be-

[27] *Checking Your Benefits in the Colorado Springs Public Schools.* Brochure of
District 11 (El Paso County, Colo.: Board of Education, n.d.), p. 9.
[28] "Mill and Factory Survey of the Month," *Mill and Factory,* 61 (August,
1957), 67–68.
[29] Ray Vicker, "Fringe Fun," *The Wall Street Journal* (January 23, 1957),
pp. 1, 15.

cause the regular school facilities, equipment, and resources are the very ones needed to operate a comprehensive recreational program.

A physical recreation program, for example, including both team and individual activities, can be initiated by using the school swimming pool, camping sites, athletic fields, gymnasium, and assorted school-owned sports equipment. Social recreational opportunities can be developed by using the gymnasium for dancing and other large group activities, the school kitchen and cafeteria for food service affairs, school homemaking facilities for small group socials, shops and laboratories for hobby development, and the school-owned musical instruments for personal practice and enjoyment. Cultural recreational activities are among the easiest for the district to sponsor. Instruction in a host of subject fields may be offered by staff members who are paid for this service by the school district. The school recording equipment, stage, and auditorium are key facilities for instruction in the performing arts. The development of book review clubs and study groups can be encouraged through use of school library resources, including exhibits, picture collections, displays, etc., which are frequently available to the school from state libraries and other agencies. Finally, the district can promote cultural recreation by providing the staff with school transportation to cultural events and institutions located either within or outside of the school district.

The fact that districts generally fail to sponsor recreation for teachers is probably not a matter of cost or of opposition to the specific activities. Instead, these districts probably believe that teachers are not interested in school-sponsored recreation, that they have ample recreational opportunities in the community, or that teachers already associate too much with one another. While each of these points may have some merit, it is unwise for a district to accept them without some verification of their accuracy. By no means should a district push a recreational program on a disinterested staff, nor should it duplicate recreational opportunities available to teachers through other community organizations. To do either would be a waste of time, money, and community effort.

There is, however, a simple way for a district to determine the recreational interests and needs of its teachers: it can ask them. One clue that school-sponsored recreational provisions may frequently be desired is found in the comment that there are few recreational opportunities available in the community, or at least few teachers can afford.

Opportunities in the community.   One effective means a community has to attract and retain good teachers is to make community living appealing to them. A community can partially accomplish this by offering teachers a variety of recreational activities. A community should be alerted by district administrators and policy-makers to the specific services it can offer, to the contributions which can be made by private community organizations, clubs, and agencies, and to the opportunities which may be possible through the joint efforts of the school district and community agencies. The degree to which the school district succeeds in promoting community support and community recreational opportunities for teachers is of crucial importance, especially to the school system.

Participating in recreation provided by community organizations immediately broadens teachers' contacts. They have the opportunity to meet community residents other than the parents of their pupils. These contacts may increase their interest in the community and the community's understanding of the school. Certainly they provide teachers with a chance to develop friendships outside of the teaching profession.

Local physical recreational resources are sometimes community owned, sometimes privately owned, and in many communities the facilities are both public and privately owned. These frequently include golf courses, tennis courts, swimming pools, ice skating and roller skating rinks, bowling lanes, riding stables, gymnasiums, skeet ranges, and hunting, fishing, and boating facilities. When these are privately owned, the school district should encourage owners to offer teacher memberships. When these are publicly owned, teachers should be encouraged to use them. Local agencies such as the YMCA, YMHA, YWCA, and YWHA should specifically invite teachers to use their facilities. Teachers should also be asked to participate in community athletic leagues which are often sponsored by local civic organizations and local recreation departments.

Civic and social clubs are found in almost every community. Some of these are chapters of national organizations. The school district can promote teacher membership in these organizations by informing the organization's local officers of teachers who have belonged to their organization in other communities, by making provisions for teacher members to attend meetings scheduled during the school day, by encouraging the organizations to invite teachers as guests to their programs, and by suggesting that the organizations sponsor special events specifically for teachers. Events might range from banquets and dances to weekend camping trips and air tours. Among the most active community groups in many locations are the alumni groups of colleges, fraternities, and sororities. The school district should not overlook these opportunities for teachers who are eligible for membership.

Communities large and small are currently offering adult education courses in a multitude of subjects. Many of these courses are scheduled, housed, staffed, and financed by the local school district; many others are offered by non-profit community agencies or special interest groups. Irrespective of sponsorship, teachers should be informed of the offerings. If the school district sponsors the courses, it may be possible for the board to enact a policy making the courses tuition-free for teachers. When sponsored by other agencies, reduced rates may be obtained for teachers; or, local businesses, foundations, or industries may underwrite the teachers' fees.

Local art galleries, museums, historical shrines, and the like offer another type of cultural recreation. Teacher visitation to these institutions can be encouraged by providing low or free admission or a season pass at minimum cost. These institutions occasionally invite local citizens to display paintings, sculpture, ceramics, photography, wood-work, and so on. Teachers should be invited and encouraged to present their works as well.

Finally, attention should be directed to the recreational opportunities afforded by local little theatre groups, community concert and lecture series, professional stage presentations, and the motion picture theatres. Those which encourage local talent provide an excellent opportunity for teacher participation. Those which are professionally presented can be made more attractive for teachers by ticket discounts and special subscription benefits.

CHAPTER III

Working Conditions and Environment

Teacher performance is the key to quality education in any school district. The relationship of working conditions to teacher performance was succinctly presented in the Thirty-Third Yearbook of the American Association of School Administrators:

> It is almost impossible to conceive of a satisfactory and effective program of education being offered except by teachers who, by and large, take considerable satisfaction in their work and in the conditions under which it is performed.[1]

Unfortunately, school districts generally have not shown enough concern for the morale or working conditions of teachers. Whether this is due to an erroneous assumption that the performance of professional personnel is not affected by the working environment or from a general apathy concerning the quality of teaching is an issue to be resolved elsewhere. The concern here is on policies and practices which produce satisfying working conditions and good morale. The teachers' working environment is the composite of provisions and conditions established by contractual agreements, administrative practices, physical surroundings, instructional assignments, professional development opportunities, and community influences.

Contractual Agreements

Most states have statutes mandating that teachers be employed by written contracts. Nine require local school districts to use a state adopted contract form. A contract form is provided for the optional use of districts in 17 other states.[2] Even when there is no state man-

---

[1] *Staff Relations in School Administration,* Thirty-Third Yearbook, American Association of School Administrators (Washington, D.C.: National Education Association, 1955), pp. 15–16.
[2] *The Teacher and the Law,* School Law Series, Research Monograph 1959–M3 (Washington, D.C.: Research Division, National Education Association, 1959), p. 44.

date, districts generally require written contracts at least for the initial period of employment.

While it is agreed that a written contract is desirable because it states in legally enforceable terms the conditions accepted by the parties involved, the fact is that neither state nor locally-devised teacher contracts indentify in any detail the specific conditions agreed to by the contracting parties. Rarely does a teacher's contract contain a detailed statement of the instructional obligations, non-teaching duties, official hours, pay procedures, tenure and dismissal policies, or retirement provisions of the school district. Yet all of these are issues of importance to both parties. Without such detailed information teachers may not realize what is expected of them or provided for them.

It would be well for each school district to state in clear and specific written form the policies, rules, and regulations which affect the working environment of the staff.

Board rules and regulations. Many boards of education supply each of their teachers with a copy of the district's personnel policies; however, investigations indicate that a large number of teachers are in districts which do not render this service. When 1973 urban districts were surveyed in 1955 only 1063, or approximately 54 per cent, reported that they supplied each of their teachers with a copy of their personnel policies and regulations.[3] More recent informal surveys have yielded similar results.

Districts supplying printed personnel policies and regulations follow no standardized pattern. Their materials vary in quantity and physical format. They may be labeled District Policies; Policies, Rules, and Regulations; Regulations and By-Laws; or Principles and Practices. As a general rule, the content will include provisions for some or all of the following: (1) employment processes, (2) job requirements, (3) salary and other financial benefits, (4) professional growth opportunities, and (5) transfer, promotion, and separation procedures. When such additional information as staff rosters, school system forms, and administrative procedures are included, these publications are more often labeled Staff Manuals, Teachers Handbooks, or Administrative Guides. Irrespective of ti-

---

[3] *Teacher Personnel Practices, Urban School Districts, 1955–56,* Special Memo (Washington, D.C.: Research Division, National Education Association, June, 1956), p. 4.

tle, these documents vary from collections of several mimeographed or printed sheets stapled to the contract form to volumes of 200 or more pages with spiral or stitched bindings. Some are commercially printed while others are prepared within the central office of the school district or in one of the district's vocational departments.

Although it is imperative for each school district to formally adopt written personnel policies, rules, and regulations, it is equally imperative for each teacher to be provided with copies of them. Districts invariably fall short of their goal when they rely on the staff's becoming and remaining informed about personnel policies through oral communication, through the posting of policy provisions on the bulletin boards of each school, or through other similar procedures.

Salary schedules and payments. Teachers, like other employees, are interested in knowing what they will earn for their services and when and how their salaries will be paid. School districts for the most part have salary schedules which designate the pay teachers will receive. Currently 35 states have teacher salary laws which establish minimum salaries that districts may offer teachers. Many districts have comprehensive salary schedules which list teacher classifications and designate for each the salary minimums, maximums, increment patterns, and the operating principles for determining salary changes. Typical districts with schedules having these characteristics are Great Falls Public Schools, Great Falls, Montana; Ridgewood Public Schools, Ridgewood, New Jersey; Memphis City Schools, Memphis, Tennessee; and the Morrisville School District, Morrisville, Pennsylvania.

The method and frequency of salary payments can be either a convenience or an annoyance to teachers. The usual procedure of paying teachers by check is a desirable practice. It reduces the possibility of the loss of cash by the teacher and facilitates school-district bookkeeping. Checks are generally accompanied by an itemized record of the monies withheld for income tax, social security, state retirement, and other deductions. Some districts withhold, at the teacher's request, additional amounts as payments for health insurance, life insurance, dues for professional organizations, and other approved accounts.

In recent years a number of districts have changed from a 10-month basis for payment of teacher salaries to a 12-month basis. A

1955 survey of urban districts showed that 64 per cent of the responding districts provided payments on the 12-month basis. Many of these districts allowed teachers the option of receiving their summer payments in one check, usually their tenth. Sixty-eight per cent paid teachers by the calendar month or on four-week periods, while the other 32 per cent paid on a twice-per-month or bi-weekly basis.[4]

Districts differ in their procedures for distributing salary payments just as they do in frequency of payments. The four most generally used procedures are (1) delivery of checks to teachers in their schools, (2) mailing checks to teachers at their home address, (3) requiring teachers to pick up checks at the central office of the school district, and (4) deposit of payment by the district to the teacher's account in a bank of his choice. Regardless of the method used, each teacher has the right to receive his payment in a confidential manner on the day it is due.

A practice followed in a number of districts which affects the amount of pay teachers receive is that of offering extra pay for extra duties. In spite of strong arguments condemning it, the practice is a popular one among school districts, and the amount payable to an individual teacher has been reported to range from twenty-five to twenty-eight hundred dollars per year. An investigation by the Educational Research Service in 1960 showed that there has been no systematic nationwide survey of extra-pay practices in recent years.[5] However, 493 of the 554 districts responding to a questionnaire survey of school districts having a population of 30,000 or more stated that they granted extra-pay for extra duties in 1958–59. The potential influence of this practice on working conditions becomes evident when an examination of 585 salary schedules from the 724 school districts with a population of 30,000 or more revealed only 102 schedules which included any information on extra-provisions.

> In view of the fact that nearly 500 of the districts had reported granting extra pay in 1958–59, it appears that arrangements for additional compensation are frequently made individually, rather than under a definite salary-schedule provision. In some school

---

[4] *Ibid.*, pp. 22–23.

[5] *Extra-Pay Provisions in 1959–60 Salary Schedules*, Educational Research Service Circular No. 4 (Washington, D.C.: Research Division and American Association of School Administrators, National Education Association, May, 1960), p. 1.

systems, the extra pay schedule is adopted separately from the regular salary schedule and does not appear in the document provided when a copy of the regular schedule is requested.[6]

Any district that pays for extra duties should do so according to a formally adopted board policy which is known to the entire professional staff. Extra-pay policies adopted by the districts of Allentown, Pennsylvania; Pontiac, Michigan; and Abington, Pennsylvania are good examples of this recommendation.

Tenure. Usually, local school district action related to teacher tenure is guided or controlled by state statutes. At present 24 states and the District of Columbia have state-wide tenure laws. Thirteen states have tenure laws that are not state-wide in application, and the remaining 13 states are without tenure laws. There are a relatively few local systems in states without tenure which have enacted provisions to promote maximum job security for competent teachers.

The school districts of Arlington and Richmond, Virginia, are two, in a state without a tenure statute, which grant teachers a continuing contract upon successful completion of a probationary period. In addition, they have adopted teacher dismissal policies which provide that the teacher be given notice of this intention by the board, reasons for dismissal, an opportunity for a hearing, and the right to an appeal before the local board of education. The freedom to enact similar provisions is frequently within the discretionary power of the local board even in states without tenure laws.

Retirement. Teachers are covered by a state or local retirement system in all states, and in 33 states some or all teachers are included under social security. With the exception of Delaware, teachers contribute to the cost of their retirement benefits. The contributions to the joint-contributory systems differ among states as do supplemental, coordinated, and integrated dual-coverage retirement and social security arrangements.

Under most state statutes the local district has the prerogative of fixing a compulsory retirement age. This must fall within the range of the minimum age for voluntary retirement and the compulsory retirement age as designated in the statute. Some districts have accepted the state mandated retirement age as their local policy

---

[6] *Ibid.,* p. 2.

while others have established an earlier age for compulsory retirement. A third group of districts have a local compulsory retirement age earlier than the state maximum, with provisions permitting employment past the established age on a yearly basis until the state maximum is reached. The policies of two New Jersey school districts, Passaic and Tenafly, illustrate different concerns for a fixed chronological age for retirement. In Passaic:

> All teachers on attaining the age of 65 years shall be retired by the Board from the school service to take effect on August 31 following their 65th birthday. The Board reserves the right to retire employees at an earlier age (62) as permitted by State Law.[7]

In Tenafly:

> Except as may be otherwise provided in Section 2, it shall be the policy of this Board that an employee of the Tenafly School System shall be retired not later than June 30 of the school year during which that employee has attained the age of sixty-five (65) years, notwithstanding the fact that such employee has or shall have acquired tenure of office or employment by virtue of the provisions of any school law of this State.
>
> When in the judgment of the Board it is in the best interests of the school system and the employee under the then existing circumstances, the Board may defer the retirement of an employee who has reached the age of 65 years provided the Board requests an extension.
>
> The retention of an employee beyond the end of the school year during which he attains the age of 65 years shall be on a year-to-year basis but not to exceed three successive years upon the annual approval of the Board, and then only after the employee has successfully passed a thorough physical examination by a doctor selected by the employee from among at least three doctors named by the Board for that purpose so that the Board may be satisfied that the employee can satisfactorily perform the duties assigned to him.[8]

The issue of compulsory retirement for professional personnel, based solely on chronological age, is a controversial one. Those against this practice argue that it ignores the concept of individual differences, that it deprives pupils of superior teaching, and that it is both psychologically and economically unsound. Others argue that it

---

[7] *Personnel Policies* (Passaic, N.J.: Board of Education, September, 1955), p. 28.
[8] *Policy For Retirement of School Employees, Tenafly, Public Schools* (Tenafly, N.J.: Board of Education, adopted March, 1955; amended June, 1956).

removes emotional and sentimental pressures from personnel administration, creates incentives for younger teachers, and can be objectively administered. If opposition arguments are to any degree accurate, boards of education and chief school administrators should give serious attention to developing greater flexibility in their local retirement policies.

Time schedules and outside employment. The length of the work-day varies with individual teachers, and any attempt to establish a fixed number of hours or minutes for it would be disastrous; this would ignore differences in work-rates, competence, dedication, and a host of other personal factors which determine the time teachers give to their jobs. On the other hand, each district must be concerned with the hours teachers are required to spend at school and whether or not restrictions should be established on their use of time out of school.

It is common practice for districts to define the teachers "day at school" in relation to the official day for pupils. Some designate a specific number of minutes before and after the school day that teachers must be in the building. Others expect teachers to be available before and after the pupil-day for whatever period of time the teacher considers necessary. Those favoring the policy of a definite time-assignment believe that it reduces the possibility of a misunderstanding between teachers, administrators, and parents concerning the working day of teachers. Those who favor the second policy hold that professional personnel should not be regulated by specific time assignments.

The length of the teacher's day at school is influenced by the frequency and length of meetings either prior to the arrival of the pupils in the morning or after their dismissal in the afternoon. The usual district policy in this regard is that teachers are expected to attend all meetings called or approved by the central office or building administrator. Statements of this type permit the scheduling of meetings with little advance notice. Some districts, however, designate certain days and hours for meetings and other activities requiring teacher attendance. This permits teachers to plan personal activities with little or no conflict, and it helps to promote good working conditions. The following illustrate some of the better policies used by districts.

Abington Public Schools, Abington, Pennsylvania: Teachers' meetings are scheduled for each Monday at the close of the afternoon session. Attendance at all scheduled or called meetings is a professional requirement and obligation.

If it should be necessary to call a meeting at another time, each principal, supervisor, or special teacher should give ample notice and due consideration when a number of teachers are involved.[9]

Greeley Public Schools, Greeley, Colorado: All elementary and junior high schools will hold regular staff meetings each Wednesday at 3:15 P.M. The senior high school will hold its staff meetings on Monday at 8 A.M. Regular attendance at these meetings is expected of all teachers. Excuses will be considered only for emergencies.[10]

White Plains Public Schools, White Plains, New York: Generally, the following afternoons are reserved for the meetings indicated:
Monday—City-wide meetings.
Tuesday—White Plains Teachers' Association Meeting.
Wednesday—Individual school faculty meetings.[11]

District restrictions on outside employment by teachers are few, but not unusual. Current policy statements on this matter are of three types: those which strongly discourage outside employment; require clearance for employment; and limit the hours of outside employment. An example of a policy that strongly discourages outside employment is found in Hillsborough County Public Schools, Tampa, Florida. It reads:

> Teachers, supervisors, and administrators should understand that their services to the school system constitute a full-time job. Persons who accept supplemental employment understand that they do so at the risk of possible impairment of their services to the school system and place upon themselves the responsibility of satisfactory proof to the contrary. This policy is not to be construed as discouraging persons from accepting outside employment during holiday or vacation periods.[12]

The boards of District No. 3, Boulder County, Colorado; South Bend, Indiana; Jackson, Mississippi; Meridian, Mississippi; Rich-

---

[9] *Administrative Handbook and Employees' Guide* (Abington, Pa.: Abington Township School District, 1960–61), p. 57.

[10] *Handbook of Policies and Procedures* (Greeley, Colo.: Greeley Public Schools, 1960), p. 44.

[11] *Professional Staff Handbook* (White Plains, N.Y.: White Plains Public Schools, 1959–60), p. 39.

[12] *Guidebook of Policies and Procedures* (Tampa, Fla.: Hillsborough County Public Schools, February, 1960).

mond, Virginia; and Ogden, Utah require their teachers to obtain
approval for outside employment.

Limitations of the hours of outside employment are established
in different ways. Some districts specify the number of hours teachers may engage in outside employment; others establish limits on the
number of college courses which may be taken during the school
year. The end result of both provisions is a restriction on how
teachers may use their outside time. In Tulsa, Oklahoma, the position is taken that:

> . . . sometimes educational employees of the schools wish to aug-
> ment their incomes by doing part-time work outside school hours.
> Such work is permitted with definite limitations. First, the work
> must be approved in writing in advance by the Superintendent of
> Schools. Second, no full-time educational employee may work
> more than fifteen hours per week on an outside job, and no half-
> time educational employee may work more than thirty hours per
> week on an outside job.[13]

A similar limitation is imposed on teachers in Clark County
School District, Clark County, Nevada, where the regulation states:

> It is expected that no teacher shall assume assignments in col-
> lege or other outside work that will interfere in any way with regu-
> lar classroom duties or such extra-curricular duties as the
> administration may assign. It is recommended that a teacher shall
> not assume college work in excess of three semester hours in each
> semester. Certified personnel assigned to half-day teaching shall not
> accept other employment during the official school day of the po-
> sition to which they are assigned.[14]

The districts of Cheltenham and Mount Lebanon, Pennsylvania,
have provisions basically like those of Clark County, Nevada.

In contrast, the policy of the Newark, Delaware, School District
should be noted. The policy endorses outside employment for school
employees as follows:

> School employees may seek and accept employment outside of
> their regular school duties. However, the Superintendent of Schools
> may require an employee to discontinue outside employment if and

---

[13] *Administrative Rules and Procedures* (Tulsa County, Okla.: Independent
School District No. 1, 1960–61), p. 52.

[14] *Teachers' Handbook and Policy Manual* (Clark County, Nev.: Clark County
School District, 1960), p. 29.

when such employment interferes with the employee's teaching efficiency.[15]

If it is true that the primary reason teachers accept outside employment is to supplement inadequate salaries, the best solution to the problem would be to improve teacher remuneration, thereby removing the need for outside employment.

Non-teaching responsibilities and clerical duties. In the operation of every school system many routine as well as professional tasks must be performed. Among them are supervision of playgrounds, cafeteria, and buses; transcription of attendance, health, and inventory records; and preparation and production of instructional materials. Though all have their place in the administration of a school system, some are clerical in nature and do not require a professional person to perform them. Research investigations show that teachers consider clerical duties to be one of the major obstacles to good teaching.[16] Approximately 30 per cent of the experienced teachers responding in 1956 to a survey conducted by the National Education Association reported that the monitorial duties they were currently assigned required more of their time than those assigned to them five years previously. Thirty-eight per cent of the same group when asked about clerical duties replied in a like manner.[17] In 1958 the Study Conference on the Utilization of Teacher Time recommended that policies be adopted by local school districts which would relieve teachers from "handling duties which do not require professional training such as keeping records, cutting and running stencils, and doing other routine non-teaching details."[18] Having someone else handle non-teaching duties leaves the teacher more time for professional work. These and other recent studies tend to confirm the fact that teachers consider their working conditions

---

[15] *Policy Manual Newark Board of Education* (Newark, Del.: Board of Education, May, 1960), p. 14.

[16] *Conditions of Work for Quality Teaching* (Washington, D.C.: Department of Classroom Teachers, National Education Association, June, 1960), p. 49.

[17] *The Status of the American Public-School Teacher,* Research Bulletin, Vol. 35, No. 1 (Washington, D.C.: Research Division, National Education Association, February, 1955), pp. 135–36.

[18] *Classroom Teachers Speak of Utilization of Teacher Time,* Report of the Study Conference on the Utilization of Teacher Time (Washington, D.C.: Department of Classroom Teachers, National Education Association, November 28–29, 1958), p. 5.

unsatisfactory when they are assigned routine duties which they neither like nor have time to perform.

A number of districts have recently taken action to reduce the non-teaching and clerical duties of teachers. One example has been the employment of "teacher-aides." Although no standardized function or qualifications have been established for these aides, the following excerpt indicates how they are used in Waterloo, Iowa Public Schools, Waterloo, Iowa.

> Teacher-aides work under the direction of the building principal and the teachers to whom they are assigned. They do all kinds of jobs which free teachers to concentrate on teaching, but they do not teach. They relieve the teacher on the playground before school, at recess time, and at noon. Examples of some of the other jobs that teacher-aides do are: locating materials for units of work, sorting children's work, setting up a movie screen and projector and operating it during the class period, listening to those children read who have prepared special stories, inventorying books at the end of the year, preparing seatwork materials under the direction of the teacher, collecting money for milk and keeping records, collecting other money, correcting papers which can be objectively treated, recording results, keeping attendance records, writing on the board, checking library books and playground equipment, and assuming housekeeping duties.[19]

Additional practices for reducing the time professional personnel must spend on non-teaching tasks include the use of senior high school business classes for selected clerical work; the maintenance of local and state attendance records and reports by central office non-professional personnel; the establishment of typing and clerical pools to serve teachers; and, the use of selected lay volunteers to care for routine duties.

Some districts have given special attention to provisions which relieve elementary teachers of noon-hour supervisory responsibilities. Statements of practices used by 33 districts were cited in a recent National Education Association publication.[20] These range from extra pay to teachers to the employment of non-professional

---

[19] *Teacher-Aides: Current Practices and Experiments,* Educational Research Service Circular No. 5 (Washington, D.C.: Research Division and American Association of School Administrators, National Education Association, July, 1960), p. 17.

[20] *Noon-Hour Procedures In Elementary Schools,* Educational Research Service Circular No. 6 (Washington, D.C.: Research Division and American Association of School Administrators, National Education Association, August, 1960), pp. 8–17.

personnel on an hourly basis. The concern for teachers' free time during the school day has resulted in the enactment of "right-to-eat" laws in Illinois, Massachusetts, and Ohio. These laws authorize duty-free uninterrupted periods of time for teachers. Women teachers working in Pennsylvania are assured by state statute of a daily 30 minute duty-free rest or lunch period.

When it is realized that these non-teaching duties offer no satisfaction to teachers, that they adversely affect teacher morale, and that they can be performed cheaper and probably more accurately by non-professional personnel or machines, working conditions and instructional efficiency will very likely improve.

Administrative Practices

School district personnel policies are most likely to produce good morale and high quality teaching when they are the product of sound administrative practices. Important in this regard is the practice of involving the staff in personnel policy formation.

Staff involvement in policy formation.   Teacher involvement in personnel policy development is an important objective for districts interested in providing satisfactory working conditions. Authorities in personnel administration support the propositions that teachers have a right to participate in decisions which affect their personal and family welfare, that better decisions are likely to result from broad professional participation, and that teacher participation increases teacher understanding, appreciation, and support of policies which are enacted.

These propositions were supported in a 1956 NEA Research Division survey report which showed that 98 per cent of approximately 2000 responding urban school districts were using one or more procedures for securing teacher participation.[21] Furthermore, the NEA Committee on Tenure and Academic Freedom in another publication stated that "to an increasing extent personnel policies are being developed by the cooperative efforts of boards of education, school administrators, classroom teachers, and parents."[22] The Committee likewise identified one of the essentials as "personnel

---

[21] *Teacher Personnel Practices, Urban School Districts, 1955–56, op. cit.,* p. 5.
[22] *Practical Personnel Policies* (Washington, D.C.: Committee on Tenure and Academic Freedom, National Education Association, n.d.).

practices which are mutually agreed upon by employer and employee."[23] Although many districts report teacher participation in policy formation, only a few have policy statements endorsing the concept.

Perhaps the most common practice followed in local districts is the appointment of a teacher or staff advisory committee to participate in the broad field of personnel policy advisement. Sometimes called the Educational Cabinet, Teacher Panel, Personnel Advisory Committee, or Staff Personnel Committee, these committees are expected to bring to the attention of the administration and board of education matters which are of concern to the staff; to study special problems; to communicate with the staff; and to advise the board in those areas for which their assistance has been requested.

Other districts follow the practice of appointing teacher study and advisory committees to consider discrete aspects of the personnel program. These committees are organized for a specific task and then dissolved once their assignment is completed. A third practice is found in districts which submit policy proposals and questions to the entire teaching staff or to the local professional association for their opinion. This procedure has many variations but its basic purpose is to obtain total staff reaction.

A good example of a statement on staff participation in policy development is as follows:

> The Teachers Personnel Advisory Committee shall consist of twelve members, eight of whom shall be classroom teachers, nominated and elected for terms of two years by the classroom teachers in this school district. The remainder of the committee, four members, shall be administrative, supervisory, and special service personnel elected by the teaching, supervisory and administrative staff of the Ithaca Public Schools. . . .
>
> The Advisory Committee shall meet with the personnel committee of the board in October to discuss its proposed agenda and to ascertain other matters which might come under its jurisdiction for study.
>
> The committee shall discuss any matters concerned with the welfare of teachers.
>
> The committee may present matters to the entire professional staff (teachers, supervisors, principals, administrators) for its consideration.

---

[23] *Ibid.*, p. 1.

The committee shall present matters for discussion and decision whenever advisable to the superintendents and the Board of Education. . . .[24]

Grievance procedures. A grievance has been defined by Jucius as "any discontent or dissatisfaction, whether expressed or not and whether valid or not, arising out of anything connected with the company that an employee thinks, believes, or even feels, is unfair, unjust, or inequitable."[25]

Since grievances cannot be abolished, it is essential to establish procedures and machinery for processing them. If the procedures are well defined and generally understood, they can reduce the number and the seriousness of grievances which are likely to develop.

Authorities in both industrial personnel management and educational personnel administration agree on the objectives and essential elements of efficient grievance procedures. The policy should provide each staff member with the opportunity:

1. to state his grievance, without fear of reprisal, to his administrative superior;
2. to appeal the decisions of the administrative superior to a higher administrator and ultimately to the board of education;
3. to seek advice and counsel from a grievance committee, elected by the staff, concerning his presentation and/or appeal of a grievance;
4. to initiate, appeal, and obtain a final decision on a grievance within specified time limitations.

Even though these provisions have been endorsed by the American Association of School Administrators,[26] the Department of Classroom Teachers,[27] and the National Commission for the Defence of Democracy Through Education,[28] relatively few school

---

[24] *Policy 4121, Board of Education, Ithaca Public Schools* (Ithaca, N.Y.: Board of Education, November, 1960), pp. 1–2.

[25] Michael J. Jucius, *Personnel Management,* 4th ed. Homewood, Ill.: Richard D. Irwin, Inc., 1959), p. 490.

[26] *Staff Relations in School Administration, op. cit.,* pp. 60–62.

[27] *Conditions of Work for Quality Teaching, op. cit.,* pp. 93–94.

[28] *Taking the Grief Out of Grievances in Public School Systems* (Washington, D.C.: National Commission for the Defense of Democracy Through Education, National Education Association, October, 1958).

districts provide for them in their personnel policies. School systems could use advantageously as a model the major provisions of the Orleans Parish policy. One of the most comprehensive available for review, this policy statement reads:

> A grievance is a disagreement involving the work situation in which an individual or a group believes that an injustice has been done because of the lack of policy, because of a policy which is unfair, or because of deviation from the policy or the misrepresentation of a policy. The development or modification of a salary schedule is not considered a grievance.
>
> A complaint is a minor disagreement, which may become a grievance if left unattended.
>
> Employees are encouraged to present any grievance or complaint with full assurance that such presentation will in no way prejudice his standing or status with the Orleans Parish School System.
>
> Employees are encouraged to first discuss their grievances or complaints with their principal or department head who should endeavor to effect a solution. If no satisfactory solution is reached, the employee is encouraged to discuss the grievance with the Assistant Superintendent or Division Head.
>
> It is also recognized that some problems can arise wherein a teacher may be reluctant to discuss the matter with his principal or Assistant Superintendent, or his Department Head or Division Head. In such cases he may consult directly with the Director of Personnel, and may at the time, present his grievance in person or with representatives of any employee organization or other interested parties.
>
> Upon hearing any grievance or complaint, the Director of Personnel will advice, counsel, and take steps which are in his opinion necessary or desirable to effect a proper solution.
>
> Where none of the above steps offers a solution satisfactory to the employee, he may present his problem, in writing, to the Superintendent with the request that the grievance be referred to the Board of Review. Immediately upon receipt of this request, the Superintendent shall request of the Director of Personnel all information he has pertaining to the case and, in conjunction with the employee, appoint a Board of Review.
>
> The Board of Review will review all information available relative to the case and make a recommendation to the Superintendent. After the Superintendent has received the recommendation of the Board of Review, he shall notify the aggrieved employee and others concerned in the matter of his decision.
>
> If, after receiving the decision of the Superintendent in his case,

the aggrieved employee is not satisfied with the decision, he may appeal in writing for a formal hearing by the Orleans Parish School Board, the outcome of such hearing to be final.[29]

Professional organizations.   Boards of education which recognize and respect professional organizations as the legitimate agencies of professional personnel are usually sincerely concerned for the morale and working environment of their teachers. However, it is extremely difficult to ascertain the status of school district policies and practices related to professional organizations. The large majority of districts have no written policies and their practices are often inconsistent. On the other hand, there are districts which have written policies accepting professional organizations as official spokesmen for their staffs, or policies which require teacher membership in one or more professional organizations. Also, a sizable number of boards of education endorse and support the codes of ethics of professional organizations.

The range of positive support given to professional organizations by districts having written board policies is reflected in the provisions of the Detroit Public Schools.

> Employees of the Board of Education are assured, so far as the Board is concerned, and pursuant to its established policy, continuance of employment will not be affected in any way by membership or non-membership in any craft, technical, professional, fraternal or employee organization not subversive in character; further, that employees are free to join or to refrain from joining any such organization without jeopardizing their employment by so doing; also that whether they be members or non-members of such organizations, employees may continue to bring to the Board and its committee for consideration and adjustment any matter concerning their employment or relationship to the Board.[30]

Even though school district support and cooperation with professional organizations is desirable, the merits of any policy mandating membership are highly questionable. Professionally orientated individuals will voluntarily join these organizations, support their objectives, and personally benefit from their activities. But the main

---

[29] *Personnel Handbook* (New Orleans, La.: Orleans Parish School Board, 1958), pp. 6–7.

[30] *Teachers' Bulletin, Number 2, 1958–59* (Detroit, Mich.: Detroit Public Schools, 1958), p. G–36.

point is that these are private organizations outside the legal control of the school district and the district has no right to force teachers to join one or more of them.

Physical Surroundings

It is a generally accepted fact that the physical environment in which individuals work influences their productivity. The extensive efforts of the business world to improve working surroundings and comfort facilities for employees in factories, offices, and stores reflect belief in this principle. In recent years, leadership in public education has likewise exerted efforts to affect improvement in the physical work environment of teachers. At the state level, legislatures, councils of education, and state departments of education have established requirements for new school construction which protect classrooms from excessive outside noises and insure proper heating, lighting, and ventilation in all rooms. These same agencies recommend teacher restrooms and lounges; teacher workrooms and offices; and staff dining rooms or serving areas as facilities which contribute to good staff morale and, consequently, to high productivity. Local boards of education have included many of these recommended facilities in their post-war buildings.

Physical plant. While teachers differ in their concept of an ideal school building, they all agree that the school plant should be clean, well-maintained, and of adequate size to accommodate the program. A recent teacher conference on utilization of teacher time identified the physical plant conditions considered essential to job satisfaction:

> Best use of teacher time is possible when the building is adequate to house the student body; equipped with auxiliary facilities including library, health service center, auditorium, offices, teacher's workrooms, and student and teacher restrooms; and staffed with competent maintenance and custodial help sufficient to maintain maximum efficiency.[31]

Maintaining staff efficiency in schools which fail to meet these minimum criteria is difficult because teachers become discouraged and disillusioned.

---

[31] *Utilization of Teacher Time, op. cit.,* p. 6.

Classrooms and offices.   Teachers and pupils spend the major portion of each school day in assigned classrooms. Many boards of education feel that the attractiveness and healthfulness of these rooms influence morale and are using color and design in creative ways on floors, walls, and ceilings to make the physical setting pleasant for the occupants. Some districts ask individual teachers to state their preference for color and classroom furnishings. Others encourage teachers to study the aesthetic characteristics of various materials and colors and their influence on the classroom environment.

Improvements in lighting, heating, and ventilation have probably increased teacher satisfaction with the classroom environment. More and more rooms, new and old, are being equipped with scientifically planned lighting systems which supply proper distribution and intensity of light. It seems reasonable to assume that both the personal comfort and general health of teachers and pupils has benefited from the installation of heating and ventilating systems with automatic humidity, circulation, and temperature controls.

Although teacher satisfaction with the physical aspects of the classroom is probably greater than ever before, much remains to be done. As recent as 1956, 26.7 per cent of the teachers asked to evaluate the quality of their classrooms rated them as unsatisfactory.[32] Prominent among the inadequacies cited were lack of private facilities in which to work, prepare and store materials, and to conduct individual conferences. While offices and workrooms are provided in many schools for librarians, health and physical education, art, music, and science teachers, they are seldom available for other members of the teaching staff. Although a slight increase in these facilities has been noted in recent school construction, over-all efforts have been limited.

Restrooms and lounges.   Whereas a few years ago teacher restrooms and lounges were viewed as unique accommodations, today they are considered a basic part of every new school building. The new buildings have dressing areas and one or more private rooms equipped with a cot where teachers may rest for brief periods during the day. Often there is some type of a lounge area that is large enough to seat the entire faculty, and furnished well enough to resemble a club lounge. This room, in some buildings, serves as the

---

[32] *The Status of the American Public School Teacher, op. cit.,* p. 30.

pre-school, noon, and post-school gathering place for the faculty; in others it functions primarily as a coffee and/or smoking room, or as a center for professional study and professional materials. Experience strongly supports the contention that such staff rooms are a valuable asset to faculty esprit de corps.

Cafeterias. The opportunity to enjoy a mid-day break and lunch period in a peaceful and relaxed atmosphere has long been an expressed wish of teachers. Actually, it is more than merely a desired circumstance; efficient afternoon performance, job satisfaction, and the teachers' general health are enhanced by a duty-free and pleasant luncheon environment.

It is not uncommon for teachers in large schools, especially secondary ones, to have an attractive staff lunch room in which to eat and socialize. Some of these rooms are equipped with a cafeteria serving counter, and others connect with a small kitchen in which teachers may prepare individual specialties. Table service is provided in some, but the staff dining room is typically used by teachers after they secure their food from the regular serving counter in the pupil cafeteria. Schools without a private staff lunchroom often reserve tables in the pupil cafeteria for the staff or permit teachers to eat in the faculty lounge. In contrast to the private faculty dining facilities and other arrangements for teacher comfort in secondary schools, teachers in elementary schools are often required to eat with pupils at assigned tables or in their regular classroom. While practices and policies must vary because of local circumstances, a serious effort should be made to provide each teacher with clean, quiet, and pleasant surroundings removed from students.

Outside distractions. The teaching-learning process becomes more effective when certain distractions which originate outside the classroom are eliminated. Three of these distractions are noise, odor, and interruptions.

Proper site selection, building placement, and landscaping can do much to control noises from the outside. Unfortunately internal school noises are sometimes difficult to control, especially those originating in the cafeteria, gymnasium, auditorium, industrial and mechanical arts shops, music rooms, typewriting classes, or in classrooms using record players, projectors, or tape recorders. The frequency and pattern of these noises are often more irritating and frustrating than their volume. Even though pupils and teachers learn to adjust to them, the adjustment process often produces excessive fatigue. A continuous study of the problem combined with astute scheduling, room assignments, and the extensive use of acoustical materials can reduce its severity.

A more subtle obstacle to learning is odors and aromas from school kitchens, home economics departments, and science laboratories which permeate the building. These odors, whether unpleasant or pleasing stimulate the sense of smell and become a distractive influence. An example would be the aroma of freshly baked pies floating through a classroom for a period of time immediately preceding lunch. Here again careful scheduling and close attention to the ventilation throughout the building can frequently resolve this problem.

A significant distraction to the teaching-learning process is interruption by individuals external to the situation. Teachers often complain about the disruptive effect of numerous announcements over the school communications system and the visiting of the classroom by administrators, pupils, commercial representatives, and parents.

In attacking this problem, many schools post notices advising all non-school personnel to report to the school office immediately upon entering the building. It is determined in the office whether or not, and under what circumstances, a visitor will be permitted into the classroom. Many schools likewise restrict the use of the intercommunications system to certain intervals in the day for all but emergency purposes. Clearly defined procedures governing the admittance of pupils and staff personnel into the classroom after the instructional program begins have been formulated in other districts.

School districts such as Lansing, Michigan; New Rochelle, New York; and Beaver Falls, Upper Darby, and Marple-Newtown, Pennsylvania have written policies on this matter. These prohibit some or all of the following persons—parents, salesmen, agents, police officers, process servers, community representatives, and visiting students—from seeking admittance to any classroom without prior approval from the responsible school administrator. It is a duty of the teacher not only to refuse entrance to those who have not obtained approval, but also to report violators to the building administrator. It seems clear that school districts should adopt and enforce such a policy.

Instructional Considerations

It is a nationwide practice in public education to assign groups, or classes, of pupils to a teacher. Historically this plan has proven to be educationally successful and financially feasible and there is no reason to believe that it will be changed. Teachers, however, know that learning is an individual matter and are constantly striving to provide meaningful instruction for each individual pupil in the class group. Their success is, to a large measure, dependent upon the nature and the number of pupils in the group.

Closely allied to the nature and number of pupils is the influence of instructional supplies and equipment on teacher effectiveness and job satisfaction. The choice, quantity, and availability of supplies and equipment are important enough to justify consideration in written personnel policies.

Nature of pupils.   The individual differences among pupils affect the work load of teachers. They can either facilitate or retard the learning environment of the classroom. Some schools believe that learning is fostered when class groups are structured to yield a cross section of pupil differences. Others attempt to promote the learning environment by limiting the range and types of differences within each class. Common terms used to label these practices are "hetrogeneous grouping" and "homogeneous grouping."

Districts which practice homogeneous grouping use one, two, or perhaps three factors for selecting pupils most alike in terms of these selected factors: Intelligence quotient score (IQ), reading or general achievement scores, professed career interest (especially in high schools with track curriculums such as college preparatory, vocational, etc.), and chronological age. Obviously, grouping on the basis of one, or a combination of these factors, does not produce a homogeneous class; it merely reduces the range of differences in respect to selected factors.

An increasing number of schools have policies for the education of atypical children—the mentally retarded, the physically handicapped, the emotionally disturbed, and the gifted. Special grouping or placement provisions of three types are usually included in local policies. One type is to group pupils in special classes in special schools. Another is to require that they be placed in special class sections within regular schools. And the third type of provision is to enroll them in customary class sections. Irrespective of their relative merits, each type either directly or indirectly affects the pupil composition of all classes in the school.

Class size. Teachers, administrators, researchers, and professional organizations all agree that the number of pupils in a class affects teacher load, quality of instruction, and quality of learning. For these reasons, class size has long been a popular subject for research and study. Educational research, however, has not determined the exact number of pupils that should be assigned to a class. The differences in educational objectives, teaching competency, teacher attitudes, teaching techniques, and instructional equipment complicate the problem of determining the number of pupils that can be taught most effectively in a single classroom without undue strain on the teacher.

State, regional, and national surveys have revealed that teachers have a strong preference concerning class size. They generally favor 25 pupils as the ideal class and indicate that 30 pupils are the maximum which permit effective instruction. Secondary teachers consider 100 to 125 as the ideal number to teach each day and 150 as the maximum number they can teach effectively. Whether realistic or not, school districts should be aware of these preferences and recognize that if they are met there is reason to believe that teacher morale will improve. Despite teacher preferences, the median elementary class size in the United States in 1955–56 was 31 pupils.[33] It has been estimated that in 1959, 35.8 per cent of the urban elementary classes contained 32 or more pupils.[34] Also in 1955–56 the median class size in secondary schools was 26.9 pupils with 16.6 per cent of all secondary classes having 35 or more pupils. During the same year 31 per cent of the secondary teachers were teaching more than 150 pupils per day.[35] Evidence of teacher concern over the number of pupils to be taught is the fact that 88 per cent of those responding to a recent NEA survey rated the need for written policy on class size as important or vital to the promotion of quality teaching.[36]

---

[33] *The Status of the American Public School Teacher, op. cit.,* p. 55.

[34] *Class Size in Elementary Schools, Research Bulletin,* Vol. 38, No. 3 (Washington, D.C.: Research Division, National Education Association, October, 1960), p. 88.

[35] *The Status of the American Public School Teacher, op. cit.,* p. 56.

[36] *Conditions of Work for Quality Teaching, op. cit.,* p. 43.

The usual explanations for differences in class size are rapid pupil population growth, lack of teachers, insufficient classrooms, and increased costs. Perhaps a more basic explanation is that few districts have an officially adopted policy establishing the maximum number of pupils who may be assigned to classes. With no written policy to control practices, conditions such as those mentioned above become prevalent.

Districts with written policy statements on class size hold to maximums ranging from 22–32 pupils. Districts like Great Falls, Montana; Fort Wayne, Indiana; and Centennial Joint Schools, Pennsylvania, have detailed policies which specify maximum class size for various grades, subject fields, and special classes.

Supplies and equipment. Teachers need appropriate tools to perform their jobs with success. Among the most important are books, reference resources, instructional supplies, audio-visual aids, and classroom and laboratory equipment. Good instruction and satisfying working conditions are promoted when teachers have an opportunity to participate in the selection of supplies and equipment and when they receive the amount requested at the time they are needed.

Two procedures are used to determine the need for supplies and equipment. One method is furnishing teachers with a master list of items from which they may make their choices. This master list is either compiled by the administrative or business staff or developed and kept current by teacher committees. There is ample evidence to support the thesis that teachers desire and appreciate the opportunity to select the instructional supplies they wish to use.

The quantity of materials purchased for the staff is governed by the money budgeted for this purpose. Often the amount is determined on the basis of a per pupil, per teacher, or per class allotment. A small number of districts subscribe to the practice of first determining staff requests and then budgeting a sum sufficient to meet these requests. This is a superior policy, provided teachers are held accountable for the use of materials.

To be used most effectively, instructional supplies must be easily accessible. In many systems all supplies are placed in the individual classroom prior to or at the beginning of the school year. Proper storage then becomes a teacher responsibility. Individual building supply rooms are maintained in other districts. Each is stocked with the materials allotted to the building staff and withdrawals are made according to an established building policy. Many teachers favor this procedure because it offers safe storage and easy availability. Central warehouse storage is maintained in large systems with delivery service to each school on a semester, monthly, or weekly basis. When the frequency of delivery is sufficient, such as once or twice each week, this procedure is satisfactory.

Some systems not only provide a variety of instructional equipment, but they also offer assistance to teachers in its proper use. Operators are available to assemble, operate, and dismantle many types of special equipment, such as recording machines, movie and film strip projectors, and broadcasting and public address systems. In-service training programs for instruction in the operation and use of all types of equipment is a periodic service to faculty members.

Professional Development

Although it is the personal duty of teachers to improve professionally, the school district must accept the responsibility for providing conditions which foster growth. It must stimulate both the individual teacher and the staff collectively to evaluate their present performance and to seek ways and means of improving.

Helping teachers to keep alert to new developments and trends is only one of the important staff-development services school districts should offer. New teachers should be aided in their adjustment to the job; inadequately prepared teachers should be guided in their performance; experienced personnel should be encouraged to recommend improvements in the school program; and cooperative working relationships should be promoted among the entire staff. In meeting these responsibilities, districts employ a variety of general and specialized supervisory personnel and render many appropriate services.

Supervisory services. Supervision has been defined as a service designed "to give intelligent help to classroom teachers in discovering and solving their problems and to improve teaching through cooperative planning and action."[37] The extent to which school systems accept this responsibility is revealed in their policies, or-

---

[37] *Practical Personnel Policies, op. cit.,* p. 3.

ganizational structure, and duty assignments. A review of these considerations indicates that although the range among districts is great, the majority accept supervision as a major responsibility.

The responsibility for system-wide supervision in every district rests with the chief school administrator. Within individual buildings it is generally assigned to the principal. Both of these administrators function as general supervisors with the assigned task of helping teachers. Their most common services include assisting individual teachers and groups of teachers with instructional problems, supplying the staff with adequate and appropriate instructional materials, promoting in-service growth opportunities for teachers, and coordinating the individual efforts of the staff to produce a superior educational program. Districts such as Altoona, Pennsylvania; Greeley, Colorado; South Bend, Indiana; Norfolk, Virginia, and others list these or similar services in their job descriptions for positions of chief school administrator and principal.

There are, of course, districts which assign general supervisory responsibilities to other line administrators, such as assistant superintendents and assistant principals, but lack of standardization in job title and job function for these positions makes it impossible to describe their roles.

Specialists, or special supervisors, assist most administrators with their supervisory function. While it is true that teachers in many districts have only limited access to specialized help, locating a system totally without the services of specialists would be no easy task. Districts offering a minimum of specialized services rely primarily on the available assistance of the intermediate school district or the state department of education. Others provide only those services which can be jointly financed and shared among neighboring districts. The better districts, however, employ an array of specialists, with some assigned to work on a district-wide basis and others to work with individual schools.

To list the specialists employed would be a useless if not impossible task. Job titles and functions differ according to organizational structure. But it is possible to classify the more common special services provided. These include assistance in: (1) subject fields (art supervisor, reading supervisor, science department head, etc.); (2) levels of education (supervisor of primary education, elementary school helping teachers, supervisor of junior high school education, etc.); (3) types of organization and instruction (core curriculum supervisor, supervisor of team teaching, supervisor of special education); (4) technical service areas (director of research, coordinator of testing, coordinator of audio-visual materials); (5) curriculum development (director of instruction, curriculum coordinator); (6) physical and mental health (nurses, doctors, speech and hearing specialists, psychologist, psychiatrist, etc.); (7) counseling and guidance (guidance director, counselors, etc.).

In-service growth opportunities. School districts which are anxious to develop and maintain an outstanding educational program help teachers to learn and grow on the job. Their procedure is to provide in-service activities appropriate to the needs of the staff. An excellent example of a policy statement on in-service education is that of the Arlington County Public Schools, Arlington, Virginia. It reads:

a. *Policy*

The Arlington County School Board encourages in-service training programs designed to improve the capabilities of all employees. Specific objectives of such programs follow:

(1) Increase competence of new employees through appropriate orientation on mission of the schools, the administrative organization and the specific duties of the employees.

(2) Attain and maintain efficient employees' performance in current assignments.

(3) Develop required ability and skills to utilize new methods, materials and equipment.

(4) Broaden employee skills and knowledge and develop employees for higher level duties in accordance with needs of the schools' operation.

(5) Minimize accidents, injuries, losses from errors, spoilage and waste, and decrease employee turnover.

(6) Increase management competence at all levels.

b. *Responsibility*

Continuous attention will be given by all levels of staff and supervisory officials to identify needs for employee development. All contemplated in-service programs will be coordinated with the Personnel Office.[38]

---

[38] *Personnel Policies and Procedures* (Arlington, Va.: Arlington County Public Schools, 1958), p. 46.

Districts vary in type and scope of in-service offerings and also in the methods by which they are operated. Some are specific activities, others are practices and procedures which promote growth indirectly. Those listed most often in policies, regulations, and handbooks of districts include:

1. Orientation and induction programs for new teachers;
2. Individual and group conferences;
3. Professional staff meetings;
4. Evaluation and self-appraisal systems;
5. Visitation privileges within and outside the district;
6. Attendance at conventions and professional meetings outside of the system;
7. Institutes and workshops;
8. Sabbatical leave provisions;
9. School and district committee work experience;
10. Credit for study in an institution of higher education.

Others that are described less frequently include:

1. Provisions for professional writing;
2. Exchange of teaching opportunities;
3. Partial or total tuition reimbursement for advanced study in an institution of higher education;
4. Locally developed or sponsored professional growth courses with credit option;
5. Research and experimentation grants;
6. Professional counseling services, including medical;
7. Professional library facilities;
8. Facilities for a curiculum laboratory and instructional materials.

Community Influences

The community has always influenced teacher responsibilites and teacher rights. For years, "contracting to teach" included a stated or implied assent to perform a variety of community services and to surrender many of the rights accorded the average local citizen. This is no longer the general situation. Communities are increasingly granting professional status to teachers and according them the same personal freedoms that other citizens enjoy.

Standards of conduct.   Both the profession and the community have expectations concerning the professional and personal conduct of teachers. Those of the profession are stated in the codes of ethics of national, state, and local educational associations. Those of the community are identified in the official policies of the local board of education. A study of both ethical codes and local board policies reveals a somewhat general agreement on the conduct prescribed for teachers.

In the large majority of cases, local board policies state that the staff is expected to adhere to professional and personal conduct standards established in the code of ethics of the local, state, or national Education Association. Frequently this is the only policy on the professional and personal conduct of teachers.

Additional professional conduct policies, sometimes found in local districts, place restrictions on selling reference books and educational materials, releasing confidential pupil and school information, acceptance of gifts, tutoring for remuneration, and the presentation of controversial issues in the classroom.

Some boards of education have policy statements on specific aspects of the personal conduct of teachers. These are probably considered necessary to supplement the board provisions on personal conduct found in most codes of ethics. Most of these statements focus on dress, personal appearance, intoxication, smoking in the school, personal debts, and outside employment. With the possible exception of off-duty employment, it is unlikely these requirements are any different from those imposed on all citizens. Supporting this thesis is the fact that only 2.1 per cent of the teachers polled in the 1956 NEA teacher-status study felt that serious restrictions were placed on their personal lives because they were teachers.[39]

Time and money demands.   All evidence indicates that teachers support nonpartisan community activities and agencies as much as other adults. In fact, they are more active in this regard than most citizens. In some communities, unfortunately, sundry organizations and institutions make heavy demands on their free time and bring pressure for financial support.

The only specified non-school time most districts require of teachers is attendance at meetings of parent-teacher associations and similar groups. No demands of a financial nature are prescribed. There are a minority of districts, though, in which teachers are urged to support community-wide charitable appeals, such as the

---

[39] *The Status of the American Public-School Teacher, op. cit.,* p. 33.

United Fund and the Community Chest, on grounds that teachers should "display an active interest in the community."

Although the host of pressures teachers receive to sponsor, direct, manage, or financially support cultural, civic, religious, welfare, and charitable work carry no official board endorsement, they often feel that it is necessary to demonstrate their interest in these worthy causes. As a result, they often grant more time and money to these causes than they should. Here is a problem on which much constructive action could be taken by administrators and boards of education.

Housing.   Teachers are generally free to choose their domicile. The once common policy of mandating residence within the district is relatively obsolete. Freedom of choice, however, does not always solve the teacher's task of finding comfortable, convenient, and economical housing. Some communities have a shortage of good housing; others are too large for a teacher to know where to find a suitable place within appropriate rental or purchase brackets.

Many school systems accept the proposition that satisfactory living conditions promote the quality of teaching. They offer a variety of services to assist teachers in obtaining suitable accommodations. These include:

1. Supplying maps of the community which show school locations, public transportation routes, churches, libraries, recreational facilities, etc.;

2. Providing listings of real estate agencies and organizations which handle housing;

3. Developing and distributing listings of the available facilities as determined by calls from owners or through school district and PTA surveys;

4. Supplying clerical and telephone service to establish appointments with owners and agents to inspect properties;

5. Providing a tour of the community and transportation to investigate vacancies.

CHAPTER IV

Leaves of Absence

Outstanding progress has been made during the last thirty years in establishing leaves of absence for professional employees. As the term is used here, *leaves of absence* means the right to be away from work, with or without pay, as authorized under state law or in the adopted rules and regulations of local school districts. This is the result of a more human concern for worker welfare generally and of the persuasive influence of organized teacher groups on legislatures and boards of education. These bodies now accept the fact that every employee is likely to experience unavoidable causes of absence from work or to have reasons for being absent which are related to the performance of services. Legitimate leaves of absence are granted on the assumption that they yield advantages both to the employer and the employee.

Professional workers have long made the claim that they do better work when they know they may obtain leaves of absence. Their claim is supported by the observations and experiences of administrators and supervisors who point out that these workers adopt a more wholesome attitude toward the school system; that their efficiency on the job increases when relieved of anxiety over deductions in salary for necessary absences; that leaves for illness are an essential form of protection against the possible spread of disease; that extended leaves for reasons of health and maternity encourage employees to stay away long enough to ensure satisfactory recovery; and that professional-development leaves for attendance at meetings, exchange teaching, study, and travel yield highly beneficial results to the individuals and the school systems which employ them.

For these and similar reasons, most school systems have adopted policies granting a variety of leaves of absence. Some follow prescriptions of state law; others come within the framework of legislation permitting local school boards to set up their own regulations; and still others represent the power of school boards to adopt reasonable leave policies in the absence of specific statutes.

Sick Leaves

The majority of states today have laws relating to teacher leaves of absence for personal illness or injury. According to a recent report by the Research Division, National Education Association, legal provisions in 33 states and the District of Columbia contain reference to sick leave for teachers, while three other states authorize their boards of education to prescribe regulations for sick leave in local districts.[1]

Of these 36 states, 25 and the District of Columbia make it mandatory that teachers receive full pay during their absence for illness or injury. The number of days for which full pay may be received varies considerably, the most common number being ten. In several of these states, the unused days each year are allowed to accumulate, with the accumulation ranging from 20 days (Kentucky, Vermont, and West Virginia) to 180 days (Washington) to an indefinite number (California, Hawaii, and New Jersey).[2]

Eleven states authorize local boards of education to exceed the mandated provisions of the law and, in the absence of legislation on the subject, the courts have held that local boards may develop appropriate rules and regulations concerning leaves of absence, including those for illness and injury. As a result, striking variations are found in sick leave plans adopted by school districts throughout the country.

Types of plans. An analysis of sick leave plans adopted by local boards of education show that there are five principal types in operation:

1. Leave for full salary for a given number of days annually. Unused days may or may not be accumulated.
2. Leave with full salary for a given number of days annually plus an additional number of days at part salary. Unused days at full salary, or at full salary and part salary, may or may not be accumulated.
3. Leave at part salary for a given number of days annually. In some instances the teacher receives the difference between his salary

---

[1] *State Sick Leave Provisions, Research Bulletin*, Vol. 39, No. 3 (Washington, D.C.: Research Division, National Education Association, October, 1961), p. 94.
[2] *Ibid.*, pp. 94–95.

and the salary paid to the substitute, and in others he receives a fixed percentage of his salary. Unused days may or may not be accumulated.

4. Leave with full or part salary for a given number of days annually, the number depending upon the length of service in the local school system. Unused days may or may not be accumulated.

5. Leave with full or part salary, or a combination of the two, for an indefinite period of time.

    a. If with full salary, usually the total number of days may not exceed a fixed number for the entire staff.

    b. If a combination of the two, the indefinite period of time applies only to the days of part salary that come after the ones at full salary have been used.

While each type of plan has some merit, no single type can be recommended for wide adoption. The fact that local systems vary too much in organization, operation, and internal climate and the fact that there are wide differences in community sentiment regarding teacher welfare benefits make it difficult to decide on one plan. A more feasible approach to the question of developing new sick leave policies or of modifying existing ones is to look at the special features of a good many plans that are in operation and to determine which features are best suited to local needs and conditions.

Special features. Most policy statements restrict coverage to regular professional employees, although a distinction is sometimes made between substitute, probationary, and tenure teachers. The tendency is growing to include non-certificated personnel in the same policy statement, with hourly and part-time workers excluded from coverage.

Personal illness and injury are the main cause for granting leaves of absence, but frequently quarantine of family is added as an acceptable cause.

The model amount of allowable leave is 10 days annually, the typical range being from 5–15 days. A scattering of districts grant five days the first year ot employment and then increase the number either after three to five consecutive years of service or else each year until a stated amount is reached.[3] There is also a move to express sick leave allowance as a specified amount each month, as one day or one and one-half days, because employees vary in the

---

[3] See leave policies adopted in Lincoln, Nebraska; El Paso, Texas; and Port Arthur Independent School District, Texas.

number of months worked each year and it is easier for them to understand this provision.

Tremendous differences are found among local districts in the amount of unused annual sick leave that may accumulate. The range is from no days to an indefinite number, with a general average of 30, 60, and 90 days. In addition, several California districts provide liberal protection for professional workers who have been unable to accumulate much leave either because they are new employees or because they have exhausted previous accumulations. For example, in Oakland, when cumulated leave has been used, the teacher may have 100 teaching days more for leave. He receives, during these 100 days, the difference between his regular salary and that paid to the substitute. In Long Beach, this partial pay cannot be less than 20 per cent of his regular salary, while in Los Angeles and San Diego the partial pay is fixed at one half of the regular salary during the 100-day period.

Provisions are made in some districts for teachers to receive compensation for days of absence beyond those allowed and/or which have accumulated. In El Paso, Texas, "an employee whose pay has been reduced because he has not earned sufficient sick leave to cover the absence will be refunded that amount at the end of the year if he has earned sick leave at the time to cover the absence."[4] San Francisco, California, provides that when a teacher's illness extends beyond the amount of days accumulated for leave, he shall receive his regular pay minus a deduction for part payment of the substitute. The allowable payments for illness are limited to a total of five months in any one school year. In Santa Fe, New Mexico, the salary received during illness beyond the cumulative maximum is the difference between the regular salary and what is paid to the substitute. Abington, Pennsylvania, allows 60 per cent of the regular salary for 15 days beyond those accumulated and 40 per cent of the regular salary for 30 days beyond the 15 in cases of continued illness. Such provisions further protect the welfare of the teachers, providing the sick leave policy has a liberal accumulative feature.

Most plans today include provisions for reducing and preventing abuse of sick leave privileges. The teacher may be required to state the reason for absence in writing and have the statement approved

---

[4] *Handbook for Teachers* (El Paso, Tex.: Superintendent of Schools, 1958), p. 9.

by an immediate superior, a school nurse, or a school medical officer. In some instances a doctor's certificate may be demanded to justify the absence even though it is only for a day or two—a practice that is rapidly disappearing. Many boards of education reserve the right to have the absent employee examined either by a school medical officer or by a private physician, and some go so far as to require a doctor's certificate for a consecutive absence of more than three, five, or seven days.

In cases where the teacher's illness or injury continues over the summer into the next school year, the question of eligibility for new sick leave benefits must be considered. This problem is handled in three ways by school districts: (1) eligibility is not permitted until the teacher returns to work; (2) eligibility is granted on the assumption that the teacher holds a continuing contract and is, therefore, entitled to additional benefits; or (3) the matter is left to school board discretion, with due regard for a physician's report and the teacher's length of service, competence, and value to the school system.

Practically all districts grant extended leaves of absence for serious personal illness or injury. The request for such leave must be submitted in writing and accompanied by a medical report. If the leave is for a semester or a year, it may be extended for another year at board discretion. Usually, no salary is paid during the period of extended absence, though Shorewood, Wisconsin, pays up to one thousand dollars a year to teachers who have been in the system at least ten years. The payment, however, may not exceed the difference between the regular salary and that received by the substitute. The rule is well established in many districts that no leave beyond the original one will be honored unless a request for a further extension is made before a specified date. The leave is automatically cancelled if the teacher fails to notify the system of his intention to return to teaching or has not filed a request for a further extension. In most districts a teacher on extended leave status has no guarantee that he will be able to come back to the position he held before leave was taken. Many districts require a complete medical examination, at their expense, before the teacher may report for work, while others are willing to accept a physician's certificate that the teacher is physically able to return to duty.

Besides the principal features just described, the following miscellaneous provisions are contained in some local district plans: Probationary teachers are either granted the same number of days annually as tenure teachers or one-half the amount. Part-time teachers are allowed a number of days in proportion to the contract basis on which they serve. Substitute teachers who are employed for long continuous periods of time enjoy the same annual allowance as regular teachers, but their unused days are not cumulative. No sick leave benefits are granted to emergency substitute teachers.

Holidays and weekends occurring during the period of absence are charged in some districts against current or cumulative leave. A teacher who is elected after the school year has started is allowed one day or a fraction of one day for each month remaining in the school year. As a rule, accumulated leave is forfeited upon termination of employment, but exceptions are sometimes made for teachers who are eligible to retire; they receive either full or partial salary payment, at their present rate, for the days with which they are credited.

It should be apparent from this review that several important factors must be considered and weighed carefully in drafting a sick leave plan. The plan will be better understood and respected if it is clearly and definitely stated in writing and kept separate from other types of leaves. It should represent a means of protecting and furthering staff welfare rather than a reward for service rendered. Costs associated with the plan can be reduced when a high level of physical fitness is a requirement for employment and when periodic medical examinations are scheduled thereafter. Certainly every plan should be liberal enough in its financial provision so that teachers who are ill or injured will not worry about economic insecurity.

Maternity Leave

The necessity for granting maternity leave has continued to grow with the increased employment of married women teachers. As a consequence, boards of education in districts of all sizes have provided for this type of leave in their personnel policies. A few, however, still refuse to accept the idea that married women with children can be competent teachers, or else they reserve the right to grant or refuse maternity leave, depending upon what they think is in the best interest of the school system.

Regulations governing maternity leave differ in some details among local districts. Eligibility for leave is generally limited to teachers who have passed the probationary period or who have received tenure. El Paso, Texas, on the other hand, permits any teacher to apply for leave if her services have been satisfactory and if she has taught for at least nine consecutive months in the system immediately prior to her application for leave.[5]

Generally, application for leave must be made in writing by the end of the third or fourth month of pregnancy. The teacher may then continue to work through the fifth or sixth month or take her leave within three or four months of the expected birth of the baby. Failure to report pregnancy or to accept leave is usually regarded as sufficient ground for terminating the teacher's contract.

The leave is customarily granted without pay for a period of one year and may be extended for a second year. Requests for extension are approved by the superintendent or by the board of education upon the superintendent's recommendation.

Regulations vary considerably on the question of when the teacher may return to work. The time may be stated as thirty days, three months, four months, six months, eight months, the beginning of the next school year, or at the discretion of the board. Ordinarily, an earlier return is allowed if the baby does not live. Practically all systems require the teacher to undergo a medical examination and be declared fit to resume her duties before reinstatement is approved. If a request for return from leave is not filed before a stated expiration date, the teacher is considered to have resigned.

There appears to be wide agreement in local district rules and regulations that a teacher on maternity leave has no guarantee of returning to the same position held when the leave was granted. She may be returned to her former position if a vacancy exists or to another for which she is qualified. In the event that no position is available, the leave may be extended until one opens, or her employment may be terminated at the beginning of the next school year.

Maternity leave also raises questions about sick leave allowance, salary steps, tenure rights, and retirement. Oakland, California, allows ten days compensation for normal delivery of the child but

---

[5] *Ibid.*, p. 11.

does not charge this against sick leave time. The policy provides further that "complications of pregnancy and delivery are considered the same as any other illness and are compensated for under the rules governing absence due to illness."[6] In contrast, most school systems do not permit sick leave time to be used for illness caused by pregnancy. With regard to salary increments, prevailing practice is to reinstate the returning teacher at the salary step held before the leave was taken. Tenure rights are usually protected during maternity leave, and the leave may be counted as service for eligibility under retirement laws, although details on this point differ among the states.

Professional Development Leaves

Leaves for professional development include sabbatical, extended, attendance at meetings, school visitations, exchange teaching, and service in professional organizations. The leaves may be for a year or more or they may be for a single day. Their purpose is to increase professional knowledge and skill as well as personal worth and value to the school system.

Sabbatical leave. Sabbatical leave is considered an effective means for encouraging and stimulating teachers and administrators, after several years of satisfactory service, to take a half or a full year away from their regular work for study, travel, cultural pursuits, or health improvement.

Eighteen states and the District of Columbia have enacted laws on sabbatical leave. These laws usually guarantee the teacher his former position after the leave or one like it, and consider the leave time active service for retirement purposes.

In a 1961–62 survey of 234 school districts having pupil enrollments of 12,000 or more, sabbatical leave is provided in 129 or 55 per cent of the districts. Thirty-seven per cent do not pay any salary during the leave period, 57 per cent pay one-half of the teacher's regular salary, and the remainder pay only a fraction of the annual salary.[7]

Although it is common practice to grant the leave for a semester

---

[6] *Handbook for Teachers* (Oakland, Calif.: Oakland Unified School District, Office of Publications, 1960), p. 30.

[7] "Long-Term Leaves of Absence," *NEA Research Bulletin,* Vol. 40, No. 4 (December, 1962), p. 118.

or a year (at the option of the teacher), some systems graduate the amount of leave according to years of service. For example, Minneapolis, Minnesota, allows one semester or quarter after 10 years, two semesters or quarters after 15 years, and one full year after 20 years of employment in the district.[8]

The number of staff members permitted leave at one time is generally fixed in order to preserve efficiency in the system. The number is fixed for both the system as a whole and different divisions of it. Minneapolis, Minnesota, allows no more than one per cent of the instructional staff to take sabbatical leave simultaneously, including no more than two principals and one consultant. The leaves are distributed among the divisions of the system in proportion to the number of teachers employed in each division.[9] San Francisco, California, restricts leaves to no more than two per cent of the professional staff or no more than one in 15 certified personnel in an individual school.[10]

Should the number of applicants exceed the fixed quota, the superintendent or an assisting committee must choose the teachers to whom leave will be granted. Choices are based on such considerations as length of service, efficiency rating, distribution of applicants within the system, purpose of the leave and its contribution to the school system. Those who are turned down may apply the next year and receive priority on the eligibility list.

Applicants for leave must accept the conditions set down by the school system. Not only must they file applications on or before a given date, but they must also state fully the purpose of the leave requested. If the purpose is travel, they may be asked to furnish a detailed itinerary. If the purpose is study, they may be required to submit a complete list of courses and take a minimum amount of work each semester. In addition, applicants must agree not to accept employment during the leave period or to receive any financial remuneration except that specified by the board of education or by the school code in states where sabbatical leave legislation has been enacted. They must agree, further, to return to the school system and remain in its employ for one or two years, otherwise they are

---

[8] *Personnel Practices Minneapolis Public Schools* (Minneapolis, Minn.: Department of Personnel, 1960), p. 34.

[9] *Ibid.*, p. 35.

[10] Cited in *Fringe Benefits for School Employees, Supplement No. 1* (San Diego, Calif.: Research Department, San Diego City Schools, 1960), p. 8. Mimeographed.

legally obligated to reimburse the district for all monies paid to them while on leave. California districts protect themselves on this point by requiring that each teacher post a bond if he wishes to receive monthly payments during leave, or else he will receive his money in two annual installments after his return to the school system.

Some school systems pay the teacher the difference between his regular salary and that paid to the substitute. Even though this difference may not be much, a ceiling is used in some districts. In Pennsylvania this restriction has been enacted as a state law. The result, of course, is that only a few of the eligible teachers can afford to take sabbatical leave. Another practice is to pay the teacher one-half of his regular monthly salary during each month of leave. This arrangement makes it possible for more teachers to take advantage of leave opportunities without as much financial hardship.

Other provisions found in sabbatical leave policies are (1) that the teacher shall return to the position he held previously, (2) that the teacher shall supply a summary report of his activities and their worth to the school system, (3) that the teacher shall receive salary increases as though leave was not taken (in some districts the increment is withheld if his salary is above that indicated in the state schedule), and (4) that the teacher shall retain his status in the retirement system according to prescribed regulations.

Extended leave. Extended leave, for a semester or a year, is granted to teachers who have tenure, subject to permission from the superintendent and approval of the board of education, with possible renewal for another year. It carries no financial compensation. Reasons for extended leave are health, study, travel, research, family illness, and others of more unusual character. Although employment during leave is prohibited, special opportunities in business, government, and education may be looked upon favorably if it can be shown that the school system could profit from the experience gained by the teacher.

Salary increments, adjustments in salary schedule, and retirement credit are not usually applicable to teachers on extended leave, nor is a particular position held open for them. On returning to the school system, they are placed in any position that is available and in which they are qualified.

Attendance at meetings. All reputable school systems permit teachers to attend conferences, conventions, clinics, workshops, study groups, and similar meetings. They consider these meetings to be valuable to the professional improvement of teachers and in keeping them up-to-date on field developments.

Teachers who wish to attend professional meetings are required to make written application on or before the dates specified in the official school calendar. Under board authority, the superintendent may approve or reject applications and limit the number approved for any one meeting or the cumulative number for the year. In many systems, those who receive leaves to attend certain meetings may not reapply for the following year or longer.

Three different methods are most often used in dealing with costs that arise because of teacher absence to attend meetings. First, teachers are permitted to take leave for a day or two without salary loss if their classes are covered by other teachers in the building and if it is not necessary to employ substitutes. Second, substitutes are employed for the teachers on approved leave and no deduction is made in salary because the cost of substitutes is borne by the district. And third, the district not only carries the cost of substitutes but also reimburses teachers for expenses incurred in attending meetings. The district may, however, limit the amount of reimbursement for particular meetings.

Several school systems charge the cost of substitutes and other expenses in their budgets as instructional improvement or in-service education.

School visitations.   School systems have continuously supported the policy of allowing teachers to have at least one or two days annually to visit other schools in or outside of the local district. Granted without loss of pay, school visitation leaves have been looked upon as a desirable feature of in-service or supervisory programs.

Exchange teaching.   With the enactment of the Fulbright Act and the Smith-Mundt Act, more and more school systems have been adopting policies for foreign and domestic exchange teaching. An example of such a policy is that of Santa Fe, New Mexico. The policy reads:

> The Board of Education, upon the recommendation of the Superintendent, shall grant a leave of absence of not more than two semesters for exchange teaching.

The applicant shall submit for advance approval, by the Superintendent, a plan for an exchange of teaching services which will outline the possible benefit to the applicant and to the school system. A final report shall be filed with the Superintendent upon return from leave of absence for exchange teaching.[11]

When the salary of the teacher on exchange is paid by the district, deductions are made for retirement. But if the salary is not paid by the local district, the year is credited to the teacher only if he or she makes regular contributions to the retirement fund on the dates required.

Services in professional organizations. When teachers are elected to positions of office in professional organizations, receive appointments to committees within these organizations, or are asked to represent an organization at some function or to serve on an evaluating committee for an accrediting association, problems arise that must be covered in the leave policy.

An analysis of leave policies shows rather general agreement on releasing teachers for services in professional organizations, but sharp disagreement on how costs shall be met for services in outside organizations.

For example, the Abington Township Public Schools, Pennsylvania, permits professional leave, or absence from duties, without loss of pay. Teachers who hold office in the association sponsoring the convention have their expenses paid by the Township. Each leave must have the written approval of the superintendent of schools.

In Seattle, Washington, the leave policy recognizes the need to release teachers who are serving as officers in national and regional organizations or who are taking a significant part in a conference program. They are permitted to attend without salary deduction, but they must pay their own expenses. If they are official representatives of professional organizations at a legislative hearing, for example, or at a state-wide parent-teacher symposium, there is no salary deduction for the absence, providing the teacher or the organization represented reimburses the district for the cost of the substitute. This rule applies to speaking engagements or similar service activities that are approved by the superintendent.

---

[11] *Policies and Regulations School District C-CA* (Santa Fe, N.Mex.: Director of Personnel, 1958, p. 15. Mimeographed.

An acute issue that is raised under the policy is how often the teacher should be permitted leave to work for a professional association. Few systems have specific rules or regulations in point since they prefer to deal with each case separately to decide what is in the best interest of the teacher, the school system, and the profession.

Special Leaves

It is well established by judicial rulings that local boards of education have implied authority, unless there is a restrictive state law, to grant leaves of absence for a number of special reasons such as illness in family, death in family, jury duty, and observance of religious holidays.

Illness in family. When there is serious illness at home and their presence is needed, teachers are released from duties and allowed three to five days of absence without loss of salary. A few systems permit as much as 10–15 days, but the time used is deducted from their current and cumulated sick leave allowances. In a few instances, up to 30 days may be granted at one-half of the regular salary. The tendency is growing to make this kind of leave a discretionary matter with the superintendent in respect to the duration of leave and the payment of salary, subject to routine confirmation by the board of education.

Long-term substitutes are now covered in many of the larger school districts and they enjoy this leave privilege as regular teachers.

Death in family. Leaves for death in the immediate family are granted universally and without loss of salary. The immediate family is defined as the mother, father, husband, wife, son, daughter, brother, sister, or any person with whom the teacher has made his or her home and has considered a part of the family. Usually three days of leave are granted, though some systems allow four, five, and even ten. An additional one or two days may be permitted without salary deduction if the death occurs in a distant community.

The practice is fairly general of allowing one day of leave at district expense for the death of a near relative. A near relative is defined as a first cousin, grandparent, aunt, uncle, niece, nephew, brother-in-law, sister-in-law, son-in-law, daughter-in-law, father-in-law, mother-in-law, or a grandchild.

Practice differs with regard to leave for attending the funeral of a close, personal friend. A full day may be granted without salary loss, a half-day without salary loss, a full day with the cost of a substitute teacher deducted, or a full day with salary deduction.

Religious holidays. Leaves of absence for the observance of religious holidays are permitted in practically all local school districts. Details differ largely on the question of salary payment. Policy statements similar to the following from Des Moines, Iowa, have been widely adopted: "Any employee whose religious affiliation requires the observance of holidays other than those regularly scheduled in the school calendar may be excused by the director of personnel without loss of salary."[12] And in contrast, many districts have policies analogous to that of the Philadelphia Public Schools. The policy in Philadelphia states that "for absence of employees due to religious holidays there shall be a deduction of one-thirtieth (1/30) of the monthly salary for each day's absence in the case of employees on ten-month basis of payment and one-forty-fifth (1/45) in the case of employees on twelve-month basis of payment."[13]

Other provisions found in local district policies are (1) leave shall be limited to one or two days a year; (2) leave shall be limited to teachers of Jewish and Orthodox Greek faiths; (3) leave shall be granted but the cost of the substitute shall be deducted from the teacher's salary; and (4) leave shall be granted and the time used shall be taken from sick leave allowance.

More and more the plans now in operation treat members of all religious sects alike. Minorities are no longer being extended privileges that were withheld earlier from the majority of teachers.

Court summons and jury duty. Present practice permits either one, two, or an indefinite number of days of absence when the teacher is summoned to appear as a witness in court. There is no loss of pay during the time specified in the policy, providing the teacher is neither a plaintiff nor a defendant in the case. All fees received for court appearance must be turned over to the school district.

---

[12] *Personnel Practices and Procedures* (Des Moines, Iowa: Des Moines Public Schools, 1960), p. 14.

[13] *Absence: Employees in the Department of Instruction,* Administrative Bulletin No. 12 (Philadelphia, Pa.: Board of Public Education, 1953), p. 7.

In the event that the teacher is called for jury duty, most local districts petition the court to excuse the teacher. They do so on the grounds that jury duty interferes with the teacher's work and that the public interest is better served by keeping the teacher in the class-room. It is for these reasons that several states have enacted statutes excusing the teacher from jury duty except during the summer when school is not in session. However, no deduction is made in salary when a teacher must serve on a jury during the school year, but the teacher is required to turn over jury fees to the school district. Here and there, districts charge absence for court appearance and jury duty to sick leave allowance.

Military duty. Laws and regulations pertaining to leave of absence for military duty have been enacted in many states and most local districts. They apply to teachers who fall within the scope of the Selective Service Act. Whether the teacher enlists or is drafted, leave is for the period of enlistment or draft respectively. In districts like Norwalk, Connecticut, the military leave policy even covers the teacher who signs a contract but is conscripted before he can begin teaching. This teacher is regarded as having had his service in the district interrupted.

For the teacher who is a reservist in the armed forces, a tour of active duty is approved only when his presence is demanded by the military authorities. Generally, reservists who customarily report for two weeks of training a year are encouraged to take this training during Easter, Christmas, or summer vacations. If they are recalled while school is in session, most systems grant fifteen days with pay. The leave time is seldom charged against other allowances—illness, injury, or personal emergencies.

A policy statement that sums up the principal considerations involved in absence for military leave is that of Lincoln, Nebraska. It reads:

1. In time of war, or state of national emergency, any full-time, regular contract employee ordered to active duty in the Armed Services of the United States, including overseas services of the Red Cross, shall, upon application, be granted a specific leave of absence.

2. This leave shall continue for the duration of the period of actual military service, and for ninety days immediately following the honorable discharge of the employee.

3. Within ninety days following the honorable discharge, each person desiring reinstatement shall so notify the Board and shall furnish evidence of physical fitness and mental competence to do the kind of work he was doing at the time leave was granted, or such other work as may be available.

4. Reinstatement of such employee shall be made within ninety days after receipt of notice that the employee desires to be reinstated.

5. The basis of compensation for a reinstated employee shall be the same as that to which the employee would have been entitled on the salary schedule for standard assignment if no leave of absence had been granted and the employee had remained in the continuous service of the Lincoln schools.

6. This does not include or guarantee any assignment in addition to, or independent of, the standard assignment or any extra standard salary allotment therefor.

7. Every possible consideration and preference in assignment shall be accorded to persons returning to the schools from the Armed Services.[14]

A number of local policies guarantee re-employment rights to the position held formerly or to one like it and they also protect the tenure and retirement rights of the teacher.

Other personal needs. Besides the leaves of absence just reviewed, a number of others are granted by local school systems in order to meet the personal needs of teachers. They include:

1. Attendance at an examination for a university degree;
2. Attendance at ceremonies to receive a university degree;
3. Attendance at the graduation exercises of a son or daughter for a university degree;
4. Paternity leave for the expected birth of a child;
5. Meeting responsibilities growing out of a disaster;
6. Visiting a husband at the port of embarkation for overseas military duty;
7. Quarantine of house in which the teacher lives;
8. Quarantine restrictions incurred in line of duty;
9. Service in a local or state legislature;
10. Moving into another house;
11. Settling an estate;
12. Attendance at a real estate settlement;
13. A wedding in the immediate family;
14. Leaving before the school year is over to take summer employment elsewhere or to undertake foreign study and travel.

---

[14] *Personnel Rights* (Lincoln, Neb.: Lincoln Public Schools, n.d.), p. 22.

Regulations governing such personal needs differ among districts. A personal leave request may be granted without salary deduction for one day a year if the reason for the request is included in the policy statement; otherwise, it may or may not be allowed. Or the leave request may be limited to three days a year without salary deduction, only if it is approved by the principal and superintendent and the time is charged against sick leave allowance. Several districts have a clause in their policy statements that all unlisted leaves shall be considered as personal leaves and salary deductions shall be made for those granted. Perhaps the soundest procedure for protecting both the interests of the school system and the welfare of the teacher is that of authorizing the superintendent to excuse teachers for emergency reasons and to determine whether or not the leave time shall be deducted from their monthly salary.

Substitute Service

An essential counterpart of leave-of-absence policy is provision for substitute service. Substitute service has as its objective that of replacing the regular teacher, though only for a day, with a person who is qualified to direct the learning process at little or no educational loss to pupils.

This means that a sufficient number of competent men and women must be recruited, screened, and made available when needed in individual buildings throughout the system. It means also that they must receive an orientation to the school system, its policies and practices, and be given whatever special training is indicated to attain the objective of the substitute service program.

The salary for substitute teachers should be high enough to attract capable people, with graduated rates according to years of service and job performance. All too often the substitute teacher receives the same per diem rate no matter how long he or she has worked for the system or how outstanding the work has been. Incentives (such as leaves for illness) for efficient service are the same with substitutes as with regular teachers.

In instances where regular teachers receive extended leaves of absence for illness, travel, study, and so on, special attention should be given to the selection of those who replace them. In fact, the same care should be exercised in their employment as the care that goes into the employment of regular teachers. Long-term substitutes should be as qualified as the teachers whose place they are to fill.

Provision should likewise be made in the substitute service policy for routine procedures, as giving notice to absence, calling of other substitutes, hours of work, evaluation of their work, and other necessary items.[15]

An increasing number of school systems are finding that the objective of the substitute service program is being realized more fully by hiring a group of qualified, full-time substitutes. They are always available when their services are needed. They are accepted by regular teachers as members of the staff, and they come to know what the regular teachers are doing and the standards they are trying to reach. When their services are not required in the classroom, they are used by building principals for curriculum projects, research undertakings, and other important activities.

---

[15] For a good example, see *Personnel Practices Minneapolis Public Schools,* *op. cit.,* pp. 53–56.

CHAPTER V

Insurance Protection

An important aspect of staff welfare is insurance and the protection it affords against unforeseen emergencies which could impair the health and economic security of the teacher and his dependents. In treating this aspect of staff welfare, consideration will be given to the needs of insurance protection, various types of insurance plans, and the means used for financing them.

Insurance Needs

As pointed out in a handbook of the Hagerstown Board of Education: "The personal well-being of the teacher has an important effect upon the quality of teaching."[1] Like this board of education, other administrators have for years recognized the fact that pupils learn best under teachers who enjoy sound mental and physical health and who are relatively free from serious social, emotional, and financial problems. It is for this reason, coupled with humanitarian motives, that the personnel programs of numerous school districts contain provisions for the insurance needs of professional staff members.

These needs are produced by the uncertainties of life and the ever present possibility of unexpected hardship which stand as a threat to peace of mind and economic security. A disabling accident or a prolonged period of illness can mean the loss of earning power. Even should income continue, it might be depleted quickly by the high costs of hospital confinement, medical attention, and surgical fees. Likewise, shorter periods of disablement from accident and illness could wipe out savings and lead to the accumulation of debts. Though the teacher himself might not suffer poor health, an accident or illness might strike a member of his family and produce the

---

[1] *Teaching in Washington County* (Hagerstown, Md.: The Board of Education, n.d.), p. 37.

same disastrous results. Of greater consequence is the prospect of his premature death which would remove the only immediate source of income and force his family to make serious adjustments in their living standards.

An infrequent but significant financial emergency could arise if the teacher committed a negligent act in the course of employment and was successfully sued for damages. Not only might his possessions be taken in partial satisfaction of the judgment but he could also be required to pay a percentage of his salary for several years to take care of the remainder.

Generally, few teachers receive sufficient income from their work to build an estate which is adequate for meeting current emergencies or for family protection after death. It would seem that the only means for guaranteeing some security for themselves and their families is an insurance program. However, the likelihood of the average teacher having enough money to purchase the kind and amount of individual insurance required for this purpose is somewhat remote. A better solution lies in the availability of lower cost group insurance.

Group Insurance

This is a form of insurance which covers a number of persons, as a group, under a single policy. Those who belong to the group are usually employed in a given business, company, or service, or they are members of an organization. The agreement entered into with the insurance firm usually specifies that a certain percentage of the employees or members of a group must join the insurance plan before it can become effective. In this way the risk is distributed over many more persons and a safer balance is maintained between those who are good and poor risks. Unless the percentage figure is attained, the probability is high that a large proportion of those who subscribe will be poor risks, and the insurance company would be paying out more in claims than it received in premiums.

Group insurance is now offered by virtually all the large insurance companies and by others that specialize to some extent in group policies. It is available for life, hospital, accident, health, disability, medical, surgical, income protection, and tort liability. It can be obtained to cover libel, slander, false arrest, false imprisonment, trespass, and malicious prosecution. Policies may be bought separately or in combination to fit the needs of the purchaser.

There are several distinct advantages to group insurance that make it attractive to teachers. It can be bought at substantially lower rates than individual policies because expenses connected with selling and administration are comparatively less. No medical examination is required, and seldom are age limits established for eligibility. Whenever a difference arises with the insurance company, the teacher is represented by the group and the issue is dealt with more effectively. Upon termination of employment, either before or at the legal age of retirement, the policy may be converted into individual insurance, though at a higher premium rate.

On the other hand, the master policy which is issued in the name of the group leaves no room for personal choices in that it must be accepted as it stands. The insurance certificate issued to each policy subscriber has no cash or loan value. The policy is regarded strictly as insurance and is for protection only. At the end of the contract period either the insurance company or the group may cancel the policy or permit its automatic renewal. Cancellation of the policy cancels all insurance certificates and leaves the teacher without protection until a different insurance arrangement is introduced and adopted.

The more common types of group insurance contracts entered into by local districts on behalf of the professional employees or by teachers' associations on behalf of their members are life, accident and health, hospital, medical, surgical, major medical, income protection, liability, or a combination of these types.

Life Insurance

The purpose of group life insurance is to provide a moderate amount of insurance at low premium rates during an individual's working years and to supplement regular life insurance policies which the individual holds or plans to purchase in the future. This insurance is issued as a one-year renewal plan, and membership in the plan is voluntary. The premium rate is usually paid by the individual teacher, although in a 1960 survey of 621 urban systems, it was found that 16 per cent of the local boards were paying part of the cost and in a few districts all of it.[2]

Eligibility. Eligibility requirements for participation in group life insurance vary slightly among the companies which underwrite this kind of policy. Generally, the contract calls for the enrollment of at least 70 to 75 per cent of the full-time, certified employees on active duty in the school district. A time limit is established within which eligible employees may enroll in the plan. No medical examination is required except for those who fail to enroll before the effective date of the policy. When an individual is employed in the district after the effective policy date, he may enroll during the first 30 days or, in some instances, the first 60 days, regardless of age or health history. Eligibility requirements in contracts with teachers' associations are almost identical.

Amount of insurance. Usually the amount of insurance that an employee may obtain depends upon his regular annual salary, exclusive of extra pay. There are, however, many contracts written in which women are limited to a lesser amount than men, the maximum for either sex seldom exceeding two to three thousand dollars. Where the amount is governed by regular salary, benefits and contributions may be changed when an employee subsequently enters a higher wage bracket.

A number of state teachers' associations have entered into group insurance contracts for their members. In Missouri, a member may buy coverage of from one to five thousand dollars, depending on age and physical health. In California, as much as twenty thousand dollars in life insurance may be purchased by members of the state teachers' association.

Premiums. The actual cost of the insurance varies somewhat with the average age of the employees who enter into the contract. It is considerably lower than the yearly premium for individual insurance.

Beneficiary. At the death of a policy member, payment is made to the beneficiary named in the application. The beneficiary can be changed at any time by the policy member, or more than one beneficiary may be listed in order of preference so that if the first is not living the proceeds will go to the second and so on down the list.

---

2 "Group Insurance Programs for Teachers," *NEA Research Bulletin,* 39 (October, 1961), 92–93.

The proceeds may be paid to the beneficiary in installments or in a lump sum as designated by the policy member.

Benefits. Group life insurance policies provide four kinds of benefits. First, the face value of the insurance is paid to the employee's beneficiary at the time of his death. Second, premiums are waived after nine months of total disability prior to age 60, and the waiver may be continued to age 65, or for life, providing proof of total disability is furnished to the insurance company each year. Third, a teacher on extended leave of absence may continue to have protection by paying the premium in advance. Fourth, an employee who leaves the school system or who retires may convert his membership in the group policy to an individual policy at standard rates.

Termination of employment. The certificate of insurance held by the teacher is cancelled 31 days after termination of employment with the school district, but the insurance may be continued on an individual basis, without a medical examination, if written application is made to the insurance company within the 31-day period. It may be converted into any type of life or endowment policy, except term insurance, or insurance that is renewed each year, and into an amount no larger than the amount held in the group life policy. The premium rate is higher and in keeping with age and occupation.

Conversion at retirement. While the privilege of converting group into individual life insurance is extended by most companies at the time a policy member reaches retirement, the amount he may convert is commonly reduced to about one-half because the element of risk is much greater.

Another method of handling conversion at retirement is that of continuing group coverage but reducing the amount of insurance annually for four to five years or until the face value drops to a fixed amount. Each annual reduction during the four to five years may be reinstated by taking an individual policy, excluding term. Premiums are at standard rates according to the age of the applicant, and no medical examination is required.

Accident and Health Insurance

Group accident and health insurance, often called accident and disability insurance, is designed to replace in part the income lost during sustained periods of disability from an accident or illness and to provide a lump-sum benefit for death or dismemberment caused by an accident. It may also have the purpose of providing financial assistance when workmen's compensation insurance is discontinued.

Eligibility requirements for certified professional workers are about the same as those for group life insurance.

Some policies are written to cover accidents that occur only on the way to and from school or while engaged during the school day in the performance of duties. Others are limited to total disability from accidents and illness arising outside the course of employment and which do not entitle the teacher to benefits under any workmen's compensation or occupational disease law. And still others, such as the one issued to members of the Des Moines Educational Association, cover loss of time due to accident or illness during the school year and during vacation periods if the teacher is confined to a hospital or to his home.

The cost of accident insurance alone is nominal, with the local board paying part or all of the cost in about 24 per cent of the urban districts, but the rates increase when it is combined with a health or disability feature.[3] Some insurance companies sell the combination at a flat rate; others gear the rate to salary classes.

The limitations found in typical policies state that no payment is made for death or any other loss which is caused by or results from intentional self-destruction, intentional self-inflicted injury, insurrection, war, or any act of war.

Hospital Insurance

Another means of protecting the economic and mental security of the teacher is group hospital insurance. Intended to relieve the teacher and his family from heavy expenses incurred in hospital confinement, it is available through several insurance companies. In the *service* type of policy, payment is made by the insurance company directly to the hospital, but in the *cash indemnity* type policy, it is made to the insured.

A given number or percentage of the eligible employees of the school district must sign up for this insurance before a policy will be issued.

---

[3] *Ibid.*, 93.

If a teacher moves to another district while the policy is in force, he may transfer his membership, assuming that the other district has a group hospital plan with the same insurance company. If it does not, then the teacher may continue as a non-group member at a higher premium rate.

Coverage varies somewhat in the policies issued by different companies. Usually the group member can cover himself; himself and one unmarried child under 19 years of age; himself and wife without maternity benefits; himself and wife with maternity benefits; or the entire family. Hospital service may be obtained from any institution of the subscriber's choice, and the service applies while traveling and during vacation periods.

Benefits begin the first day the member enters a hospital and continue for at least 70 days for each different sickness or accident. However, the type and scope of benefits vary considerably among the plans in operation today. The principal differences are found in the provisions for the number of benefit days, allowances for room and board, hospital service expenses, maternity, out-patient services, pre-existing conditions, specific diseases and pre-existing conditions, limitations for the aged, conversion upon leaving a covered group, and method of payment.

The rate of hospital insurance is adjusted to the type and scope of benefits provided. The tendency is growing for insurance companies to fix the rate schedule annually and to have it reflect the actual use of benefits. A group, therefore, that makes less use of the benefits would have a lower rate schedule, and vice versa.

Medical-Surgical Insurance

As a supplement to hospital insurance, professional employees may enroll in a medical-surgical plan the cost of which is paid in part or whole by approximately one-fourth of the urban districts.[4] An example of one medical-surgical plan is that of the Philadelphia Public Schools. Here an employee becomes eligible to join the plan after one month of employment in the system. If he joins within 31 days, he is not required to take a medical examination, but if he fails to join at that time and subsequently wishes to become insured,

---

[4] *Ibid.*

he must satisfy the insurance company at his own expense that he is a good medical risk. Should he likewise fail to include his wife and children in this application, they cannot be covered for at least three months after his request for membership in the plan.

Coverage under the plan may be taken out for the employee alone; the employee and his wife; the employee and his children; or the employee and his family. If both husband and wife are employed in the school system, each may elect individual coverage or one may choose to cover the other, but no maternity benefit is allowed under individual coverage.

The benefits included in the policy are quite comprehensive. When the employee is unable to work, reimbursement is made for a physician's home and office visits at prescribed rates, beginning with the fourth visit. Similar reimbursement is made for his hospital visits when they are not connected with surgery. The amount of reimbursement for a physician's hospital visits for each person is fixed on a per diem schedule with a maximum amount beyond which payment will not be made for any one period of hospital confinement. This reimbursement cannot be more than the amount of a physician's charges. No reimbursement is paid for workmen's compensation cases and visits related to pregnancy, dental work or treatment, or eye refractions.

Reimbursement of surgical fees for an insured employee, his covered wife or child, is fixed by schedule. The schedule indicates the highest amount that will be paid for each particular operation, such as an appendectomy, resection of the stomach, amputation of a leg, or mastoidectomy. If two or more operations are performed at the same time, payment is made for the one that costs the most. A ceiling is placed on the maximum amount of reimbursement for surgical charges for the same or related causes when operations are not separated by at least three months.

Obstetrical benefits are paid if the employee and wife are fully covered and if the obstetrical procedure occurs more than nine months after the insurance for the wife became effective. However, monies are paid for an obstetrical operation within nine months after termination of the insurance on the wife.

Further, extended benefits are provided for the employee should he undergo an operation within three months after his insurance is cancelled only if it can be shown that he was unable to work from the date of termination to the date of the operation. Medical expenses during this three-month period are payable under the same conditions.

Other insurance policies are written with benefits established for two maximum schedules—one for employees earning up to a certain amount of money and the other for those whose earnings are more than this amount. Or the policy may be divided into two types of plans, with one type costing more than the other but providing a wider scope of services and better expense allowances for various services.

Major Medical Insurance

Even greater protection against the high costs of hospital, medical, and surgical services can be procured through group major medical insurance. Written by several companies, this form of insurance applies when bills for any covered expense total one hundred dollars over and above the benefits received from the basic hospital-medical-surgical plan, though the deductable feature can be set at fifty or five hundred dollars instead of one hundred dollars, whichever is preferred. Payment is made for 80 per cent of the covered expenses as well as the expenses that are not reimbursable in the basic plan, both in and out of the hospital, up to a cumulative total of ten thousand dollars for each person covered by the policy, though a few companies set the cumulative total at twenty-five thousand dollars.

After the insured has received one thousand dollars or more in benefits, he may apply to the company for an erasure of his record so that full maximum benefits may apply again. Whether or not the company will grant his request depends upon his condition of health at the time. Payments to the insured, however, are limited to one thousand dollars in any one year.

Benefits are paid for psychiatric visits to a licensed physician while the insured is not hospitalized and ten dollars is allowed for each visit to a maximum of fifty visits annually. Benefits are also paid to cover maternity expenses incurred in the hospital beginning seven days after childbirth or miscarriage.

At termination of employment, the insurance can be converted, regardless of age or health, to an individual policy with guaranteed renewal for life. Dependents have the same conversion privilege when they are no longer eligible under the group plan.

Although the details just related differ slightly among the policies of insurance companies, the general pattern of benefits is about the same, including exclusions.

Income Protection Insurance

Group income protection insurance, also issued as group health insurance, provides the teacher with a steady source of income during periods of disability from illness and accident, especially after accumulated sick leave allowance has been exhausted. The protection afforded by this type of group insurance is evident in the policy of one company, the details of which follow.

The teacher is asked to select the amount of income desired monthly, the amount ranging from fifty to four hundred dollars. He is asked further to designate the day on which payment is to start in the event of illness. Payment may start on the first, eighth, fifteenth, thirty-first, or one-hundred-twenty-first day. The premium rate is adjusted in accordance with the choices that are made.

If total disability results from the illness, monthly income payments continue for as long as two years for any one cause of illness, and no house or hospital confinement is necessary. However, regular medical care must be received. Full benefits are also paid for illness during vacation and during authorized leave of absence when confinement is required at home or in a hospital. When the teacher is disabled without the need for home or hospital confinement, one-half the selected income is paid to a limit of twelve weeks.

If a teacher is unable to work because of pregnancy, childbirth, or miscarriage, the monthly benefit rate is paid to a maximum of ten days, though eligibility for payment does not take place for ten months following the effective date of coverage.

Should total disability occur because of an accident, income payments start on the day selected by the insured. Payment can continue for two years if regular medical care is required. If the accident takes place during a vacation period, disability must begin within sixty days after the accident. No house or hospital confinement is necessary. Actual expenses for medical and surgical care and diagnostic x-ray are also paid when bills are received within ninety days of an accident. One half of the established monthly benefit is paid if the teacher is not totally disabled from an accident or entitled to other benefits in the contract.

A principal sum is paid for accidental death, loss of both hands and feet, loss of sight in both eyes, loss of one hand and one foot, or loss of one hand or foot and the total loss of sight in one eye. One-half of the principal sum is paid for loss of one hand or one foot, and one-third for loss of sight of one eye. These benefits are paid in addition to the monthly income and are doubled when loss occurs on a public conveyance.

Moreover, supplemental payments are made on a prescribed schedule for surgery in and out of the hospital.

A somewhat different policy is sponsored by the California Teachers Association. Under this policy ten to fifteen dollars a day, beginning the first day of school, are paid to the insured member following termination of regular sick leave allowance. Payments continue up to two years for each cause of disability, but do not apply on Saturdays, Sundays, school holidays, or during vacations. The policy also provides a principal sum for accidental death or dismemberment. While the benefits provided in this policy are smaller and fewer than those in the policy previously described, the rates are lower accordingly.

Liability Insurance

Group liability insurance protects the teacher against economic loss as a result of civil law suits in which damages are awarded against him. Such suits arise because of some act or incident which causes harm to the body or property of another person and which is due to the alleged negligence of the teacher in performing his duties.

The doctrine is deeply established in common law that a school district as a sub-division of the state cannot be sued for the negligence of its agents or agencies. As a result, damage suits are brought against teachers and other employees for their tortious acts and they are held personally liable. The unfairness of this doctrine, though recognized and acknowledged by the courts, has remained unchanged except in five states (New York, New Jersey, Wyoming, California, and Connecticut) where it was abrogated by legislative action and in one (Illinois) where the state supreme court ruled against it. In these states the statutes either make the school district liable for the negligence of its employees or else authorize the use of district funds for paying judgments against teachers and supervisory personnel.

This means that teachers in the remaining states must pay damages when judgments are handed down against them unless state law allows the local district to purchase liability insurance for its employees, or the employees either purchase it themselves or procure it through membership in an outside organization. Without insurance, they are not only required to satisfy the judgment, but also to pay court costs and lawyers' fees. If they have insurance, judgments are paid up to the limit of the policy and all costs are cared for by the insurance company irrespective of the policy limit or the amount of protection purchased. Moreover, the insurance company takes responsibility for posting bond if the judgment is appealed and for securing release of attachments against the teacher's property.

An increasing number of unprotected teachers are insuring themselves against tort liability, and state teachers' associations like those in Vermont, Ohio, and Maryland have blanket policies covering their entire membership.

Financing Group Insurance

The financing of group insurance is handled in three ways: non-contributory, contributory, and self-pay. In a non-contributory arrangement, the local school district, under state authority, subsidizes the cost of the insurance. For example, San Diego, California, provides health care insurance for all employees, and employees have the right to purchase dependent coverage under the plan. Westinghouse Area School District, Pennsylvania, pays 100 per cent of the premium for group life; Pawtucket, Rhode Island, allows each employee up to twenty dollars a day for hospital expenses; and Detroit, Michigan, subsidizes the annual cost of medical-hospital insurance up to twenty-five dollars for each employee. West Mifflin, Pennsylvania, pays all costs for life, hospital, and surgical insurance as does Hibbing, Minnesota, which also carries half the cost of dependent coverage. Milwaukee, Wisconsin, and Tulsa, Oklahoma, pay for group accident insurance, while a comprehensive liability policy is supplied at district expense to teachers in Oakland, California, and Shorewood, Wisconsin.

In a contributory arrangement, group insurance costs are shared by the local district and the teacher. The amount paid by each varies among districts throughout the country. As examples of contributory financing, the El Paso, Texas, school board assumes a portion of the cost for group life; the Mount Lebanon, Pennsylvania, board carries two-thirds of the cost of a three thousand dollar life policy; and the board in Oakmont, Pennsylvania, pays 50 per cent of the group life premium and 75 per cent of the one for major medical insurance. In Racine, Wisconsin, the school board pays 60 per cent of the hospital-medical-surgical plan, including family coverage. Contributions from the board of education in Eau Clair, Wisconsin, are forty dollars for single coverage and one hundred dollars toward family coverage a year for the Wisconsin Physicians' Service Plan. The Montpelier, Vermont, board carries 40 per cent of the cost of hospital insurance and the Town of Brookline, Massachusetts, pays 50 per cent of the premiums for group life, accident and dismemberment, and hospital-medical-surgical insurance.

In self-pay arrangements, the teacher purchases his own insurance, though agreements are commonly entered into with the local board of education to deduct premium costs monthly from salary. The latter method of financing group insurance programs is the one followed in the majority of school districts.

CHAPTER VI

Benefit Associations and Services

If comprehensive teacher-welfare provisions foster high quality teacher performance, school systems profit by developing broad programs of teacher benefits. Legal restrictions, however, prohibit local boards of education from offering unlimited fringe benefits to their teachers. In addition, society restricts the benefits it is willing to finance for teachers and other public employees through tax revenue. Although welfare or fringe benefits for public employees have been greatly increased over the years, the prevailing opinion is that public employees, like other citizens, should assume some responsibility for safe-guarding and promoting their own well-being.

Long ago employees realized that by pooling their efforts voluntarily, their welfare could be promoted more effectively and on a broader scale than by individual effort. As a result, the presence and influence of voluntary organizations has become a tradition in our society.

> The tendency to form voluntary groups has been a noteworthy aspect of the history of American democracy and has given the nation some of its distinctive characteristics. Through groups Americans have developed the arts and sciences, established businesses and public enterprises, and fostered education and individual welfare.[1]

Professional personnel have organized many voluntary groups which are designated as professional associations. The operational patterns and special purposes of these associations differ considerably. However, they subscribe to two common objectives: the first is to improve the services rendered by the profession; the second, to promote the welfare of the membership.

Like other professionals, educators have established their own associations. These function on the local, state, and national level and their number and variety exceed those found within any other

---

[1] *Professional Organizations in American Education* (Washington, D.C.: Educational Policies Commission, National Education Association, 1957), p. 4.

profession. Their charters, constitutions, and platforms reflect a concern for the promotion of better education and the improvement of the professional, economic, and social welfare of teachers. The Department of Classroom Teachers has identified the role of professional associations in education as follows.

> Classroom teachers and school administrators are not different from other American citizens in needing a means of expressing their mutual concerns and professional aspirations. Virtually all Americans are now organized to provide themselves with a united voice on matters pertaining to their area of skill and specialization. The professional educator is following a familiar pattern in establishing associations to represent him. The direct participation and influence of the organized teaching profession in the development of the public-school system of the nation has been great.[2]

The largest educational association is the National Education Association. The membership of the NEA on May 31, 1961, was 765,616 or approximately 50 per cent of the public-school elementary and secondary teachers in the nation. Affiliated with the NEA are associations in each state and approximately 7500 locals spread among all the states. It is estimated that "through affiliation of the local, state, and territorial associations with the NEA, the Association represents the interests of approximately 1,500,000 teachers."[3] To promote the purpose stated in its charter—"to elevate the character and advance the interests of the profession of teaching and to promote the cause of popular education in the United States"[4] —the NEA is organized into 33 Departments, 13 Headquarters Divisions and 26 Commissions and Committees. Through the work of these agencies and the activities of their many state and local affiliates, teachers are continuously seeking to improve professional services, personal welfare benefits, and public education throughout the nation.

Psychological and Financial Benefits

The contributions and benefits which voluntary educational organizations provide for American public education and educators

---

[2] *Conditions of Work for Quality Teaching* (Washington, D.C.: Department of Classroom Teachers, National Education Association, 1959), p. 34.

[3] *NEA Handbook for Local, State, and National Associations, 1961–62* (Washington, D.C.: National Education Association, 1961), p. 3.

[4] *Ibid.*, p. 24.

are many. Often these benefits are produced through the cumulative efforts of local, state, and national organizations: therefore it is usually inaccurate to assign total credit for any contribution to a single organization. In a like manner, it is difficult, if not impossible, to separate the benefits teachers derive from actions of professional organizations into discrete categories. Some are of a specific nature and can be identified accordingly; others, however, are more general and more difficult to type.

Teacher association efforts which produce increased retirement allowance certainly offer teachers additional long-range economic benefits. For some the expanded welfare provisions will immediately provide a feeling of increased security and thereby improve their mental health. Successful efforts by professional organizations to gain tenure for teachers, to raise teacher certification requirements, and to reduce the non-instructional duties assigned to teachers are further examples of contributions which yield multi-benefits. While recognizing the interrelationships of benefits provided for teachers by professional organizations, for purpose of emphasis in the discussion which follows, benefits are classified into two types: psychological benefits and financial benefits.

Teachers, like other people, have a number of emotional or psychological needs. Some are of a social nature and primarily concern the relationships of the individual with others. Another type relates to the teacher's sense of professional achievement and self-realization. For many teachers these needs are, to some extent, satisfied by professional organizations.

These persons obtain substantial satisfaction from the relationships with others, the group acceptance, and the status-identification secured through membership in a professional association which commands community acceptance and prestige. The extensive conference and convention activities of the typical educational organization provide emotional satisfaction to a number of teachers through the display of their creative ability and professional leadership. Actions of national, state, and local associations to increase acceptance and understanding of their professional codes of ethics by boards of education and the lay public stimulates their sense of professional pride and their dedication to public service. The opportunities to communicate ideas and strongly-held educational views to a broad professional audience through publication of letters and articles in professional journals and yearbooks also provide teachers in all levels of educational work with great emotional satisfaction. Although broad in scope, these are but a sample of the numerous ways in which activities and contributions of professional organizations are psychologically beneficial to teachers.

It is generally agreed that the major financial benefits which teachers receive have been secured through the efforts of professional educational associations. In recent years the plans of these organizations have been strategically developed and applied with an acute sense of timing. Frequently they are coordinated into an integrated national-state-local program. Extensive action has been directed toward the attainment of increased benefits in a number of areas, including salaries and salary schedules, leaves of absences, retirement provisions, tenure, insurance protection, in-service education and professional growth reimbursement, and a host of additional fringe benefits.

The usual work-plan of all organizations is to establish a committee to study the specific problem and recommend a program of action. Subsequently all elements of the organization—including public relation personnel and facilities, communications media, and political contacts—are focused on the accomplishment of the established objective. With the assistance of comprehensive and highly competent research agencies (such as the Research Division of the National Education Association, the many state education association research units), and the dedicated service of the organizational membership, the endorsement of the lay-public and local, state, and national policy-makers has frequently been secured.

Types of Services

In addition to their effective work in promoting teacher welfare with boards of education, legislative bodies, and the general public, educational associations offer direct services to their members. Some teachers have a variety of services available to them, while others benefit from only a limited number. Certain of these services are most commonly offered by local teacher associations, others are generally provided by state organizations, and, in some cases, the prime sponsor is the National Education Association.

Medical services. Most teacher organizations have limited their medical service efforts to the procurement of salary replacement, major medical, surgical, dread disease, accident, and life insurance protection for their members at the most favorable group rates. In many instances, associations carry on direct negotiations with insurance companies for this purpose. A detailed analysis of teacher insurance is given in Chapter V.

Two additional medical services are sometimes provided by local associations. These are blood banks and endowed hospital rooms. Both may save teachers from financial loss, since charges for blood, or plasma, are frequently not included in insurance coverage and since insurance reimbursement for hospital rooms is often less than private room costs. In addition, both services have an emergency value. One assures availability of blood for teachers in emergencies; the other places teachers in a favored position for securing hospital accommodations when needed. Unfortunately, these services have been established by only a limited number of teacher associations.

Recent improvements in long-term preservation and blood storage procedures have enabled many hospitals to maintain blood banks. Hospital administrators are usually more than willing to develop plans whereby interested groups may create an on-call reserve blood supply for their members. In some instances the organization must supply an established quantity of blood at fixed intervals; another plan requires an initial blood supply from the organization with replacement as it is used. Hospitals in some large urban areas ask only that the organization guarantee a replacement supply to the bank within a specified time interval after a withdrawal has been made for a group member. The Spokane Education Association in the state of Washington and the La Mesa-Spring Valley Teachers Association of Spring Valley, California, have sponsored this service for several years. The latter organization offers its retired teachers full privileges in the Association blood bank.[5]

The high cost of endowing a hospital room has probably discouraged many teacher groups from considering this service for its members. Total endowments are expensive; however, partial endowments may be tailored to the resources of the group. Some organizations have created investment and trust funds of various descriptions

[5] *Local Color, 1957–58* (Washington, D.C.: Department of Classroom Teachers, National Education Association, 1958), p. 32.

in order to ultimately defray the expenses of one or more rooms. In a number of instances members of local associations have willed funds to finance hospital facilities for group members. They frequently designate the professional association, or the association and the local school system, as trustees for these funds. The Philadelphia Teachers Association is one of the few local teacher organizations known to maintain endowed hospital rooms for teacher use.[6] At present it offers four rooms to its members.

Legal consultations. A majority of state educational associations provide their local affiliates and individual teacher members with legal assistance. The benefits of this service are two-fold. Professional personnel have access to legal guidance from specialists in school law and this aid is available without cost to the teacher or the local association. Many state organizations list this service as a major benefit of membership and records disclose that teachers and local groups utilize this aid. In 1959, the New Jersey Educational Association paid more than $7500 for legal assistance to its membership[7] and in the same year legal services to members cost the Minnesota Education Association more than $10,000.[8] Early in 1962 the Maine Teachers Association spent more than $2700 in defending one of their teachers.[9]

As might be inferred from the preceding statistics, there is considerable range in the scope of legal help offered by state associations. Some of the larger bodies such as the New York State Teachers Association and the Ohio Education Associations have a full-time legal counsel as a staff member. The Washington Education Association, the Tennessee Education Association, and many others maintain lawyers or law firms on a continuing retainer basis. Other state groups employ legal assistance for each specific situation. Those which follow this latter practice generally limit their legal aid to those teachers whom the officers, or a committee of the association, feel have been illegally dismissed. At least two state

[6] *The Philadelphia Teachers Association* (Philadelphia, Pa.: The Philadelphia Teachers Association, n.d.).

[7] *What I Get For My NJEA Dues* (Trenton, N.J.: New Jersey Education Association, 1961).

[8] *Legal Services Rendered In Welfare Matters,* (Report to MEA Executive Board and Welfare Committee) (St. Paul, Minn.: Minnesota Education Association, 1960), p. 15.

[9] *Letter, Executive Secretary, Maine Teachers Association* (Augusta, Me.: January 22, 1962).

organizations, the Delaware State Education Association[10] and the Minnesota Education Association[11], have distributed to their members a guide describing legal services available and the procedure teachers should follow in requesting them.

Few local educational associations maintain legal counsel for their members. The Philadelphia Teachers Association as well as other large locals retain counsel for association business and in special situations approve counsel assistance to individual teachers.

Counseling and placement services. Education associations generally supply counseling services to their members. This is one of the major purposes for which associations are established and the basis on which their organizational structure is developed. Usually, however, it is only the national and state associations which have technically trained staff specialists to supply guidance and advice to teachers.

Teacher counseling is a major function of both the Research Division and the National Commission of Professional Rights and Responsibilities of the National Education Association. These two groups conduct research, make periodic surveys and investigations, and employ trained personnel to supply state and local organizations and individual NEA members with advice and counsel. The staff of the Research Division alone includes 20 professional specialists and 35 skilled clerical or statistical employees. Much of their counseling service is carried on through correspondence with the Division receiving an average of 1000 letters of inquiry per month. These include requests for technical information and guidance on teacher salaries, retirement, class size, working conditions, and school law. In addition, many members go in person to the NEA headquarters in Washington, D.C., for assistance.

In most states teachers also have access to counseling services from their state associations. While these services do not compare in scope with those offered by the NEA, they are particularly helpful to teachers seeking advice on state laws, policies, and procedures. Many state associations have created a Division of Field Services to counsel with local associations and individual members.

---

[10] *Guidelines For The Use of DSEA Permanent Emergency Fund* (Dover, Del.: State Education Association, 1961).

[11] *Welfare Aid Handbook,* (St. Paul, Minn.: Minnesota Education Association, 1959).

In addition to a division director, field representatives or field workers are frequently employed to assist local groups and individual members throughout the state. The state associations of Tennessee, Missouri, Virginia, and Oregon all offer their members this specialized assistance.

Teacher placement services are sponsored by only a few state educational associations and probably not at all by local associations. In most cases this is a relatively new service, although the Michigan Education Association's Placement Bureau was established in 1924. The general purpose of the placement service is to aid both teachers and school districts in employment processes. The Placement Office of the California Teachers Association has stated its function in considerable detail:

> The major responsibility of the placement office is to evaluate qualifications of candidates to meet the specifications of the school district for positions. The office assembles information concerning candidates, receives requests for referrals from employers, and arranges interviews in the CTA office when requested to do so by school officials. Placement counselors advise candidates as to the availability of positions, communicate with employers, and assume responsibility for presenting confidential papers.[12]

An additional advantage of teacher association placement bureaus is that they are usually operated on a cost basis, and charges to teachers are thereby moderate. In every instance they are substantially less than those of commercial placement agencies. Fees charged by the Michigan Education Association Placement Bureau are two dollars for registration and two per cent of the teacher's salary for the first year if placed through the Bureau;[13] the California Placement Service has a five dollar registration fee and a one and one-half per cent placement charge;[14] the cost of the Virginia Placement Service is ten dollars for registration and fifteen dollars for placement;[15] and the Oregon Association provides a completely free placement service for association members with ten years con-

---

[12] *When The Teacher Seeks Placement Service* (Burlingame, Calif.: Placement Office, California Teachers Association, 1961).

[13] *MEA Handbook* (Lansing, Mich.: Michigan Education Association, 1960), p. 26.

[14] *When The Teacher Seeks Placement Service, op. cit.,* p. 2.

[15] *VEA Handbook For Local Education Associations* (Richmond, Va.: Virginia Education Association, n.d.), p. 30.

tinuous membership, and for other members the total cost is only ten dollars.[16] In contrast, commercial agencies generally charge an initial registration fee plus five per cent of the teacher's salary for the first year.

Several state associations which do not sponsor a placement bureau offer a teacher-position listing service to their members without cost. This consists of a listing of vacancies reported by school systems in the state and qualifications needed by applicants. Both the Washington and Kentucky Education Associations provide this service.

Housing and recreational facilities. The housing services of educational organizations are of two types. The first, and by far the more common service, is local association assistance to teachers seeking living accommodations. Generally a committee, officer, or paid employee of the association maintains a listing of properties for rent or sale. This contains descriptive information about each property, the cost, and the name and address of owner or agent. Associations generally contact teachers shortly after they are employed, offer the listing service, and volunteer to arrange appointments for them with owners or agents. Some groups provide transportation so that new teachers may inspect properties throughout the community.

Several associations offer a second housing service—the sponsorship of homes or apartments for teachers. There are few of these facilities and those which do exist are primarily for retired teachers or those sixty years of age or older. At least one accommodation is maintained by a national association; state organizations sponsor one or more; and local teacher associations offer others.

The National Retired Teachers Association of the NEA has developed Grey Gables, a retired-teachers community in Ojai, California.[17] This was begun in 1954 for retired teachers throughout the United States, sixty years of age with ten or more years teaching experience. Teacher residents purchase a lifetime lease on an apartment in one of the community lodges and the entire development is administered and supervised by retired personnel.

The largest housing facility developed through the action of a

[16] *OEA Services* (Portland, Ore.: Oregon Education Association, n.d.).
[17] "Homes for Education's Senior Citizens," *NEA Journal*, 48 (May, 1959), 34–35.

state educational association is the Terwilliger Plaza in Portland, Oregon. This apartment house, completed in 1961, was conceived and planned by a committee of the Oregon Education Association and financed through the Federal Housing Authority.[18] It is twelve stories high, has 342 living units, and cost $4,300,000. In addition to the apartments, the building contains an auditorium, dining room, barber shop and beauty parlor, drug store and other commercial shops, recreational facilities, and a lounge on each floor. Apartments are available through a life-lease purchase, and monthly overhead expenses are determined on a non-profit basis.

Other state teachers associations are actively studying the possibility of constructing living accommodations for their retired teachers. Two, the Indiana State Teachers Association and the Illinois Education Association, have completed their plans and early construction of their buildings is anticipated.

In March, 1959, the Omaha Education Association and its subsidiary organization, the OEA Senior Citizens, Inc., opened a twelve-story building with 132 efficiency apartments for retired Omaha teachers and other senior citizens.[19] These units are leased for life by teachers and the plant is operated on a non-profit basis under the general supervision of the Omaha Education Association. A much smaller housing facility for retired teachers is maintained by the Birmingham, Alabama, Classroom Teachers Association.

In recent years professional associations have shown a greater interest in promoting recreational opportunities for their members. Local teacher groups sometimes maintain clubhouses equipped with lounges, library, game room, and other club appointments. Camp sites, swimming pools, resort and beach areas, golf, tennis, and other sport accommodations have been established by a smaller number of organizations.

Through the cooperative action of the National Education Association, the University of Wyoming, and the Wyoming Education Association, an outstanding outdoor educational and recreational center for teachers and their families has been established in the Shoshoni National Forest in Wyoming. This facility, known as Trail

---

[18] "Terwilliger Plaza—4 Million Dollar Success Story," *Oregon Education* (September, 1960).

[19] *OEA Senior Citizens, Inc.* (Omaha, Neb.: Omaha Education Association, 1958).

Lake Ranch, offers almost unlimited recreational opportunities.[20]

A noted recreational area maintained by a state teachers association is the 2080 acre Bunker Hill Ranch Resort operated by the Missouri State Teachers Association.[21] The property was given to the Missouri teachers in 1947 by its former owner. Since that time the Association has financed a modernization program and the construction of additional buildings. The establishment is now operated at cost for Missouri teachers by a Recreational Committee of the Association and offers a wide choice of activities.

The Michigan Education Association also owns and operates a recreational facility which includes a lodge, five sleeping cottages, a conference cottage, shop, garage, a residence, and more than 27 acres of lake-front property.[22] This was made available to the Association in 1951 by the W. K. Kellogg Foundation for two dollars and has been operated since that time as the MEA Camp. The camp is maintained as a community resource and in addition to its use by local and state educational groups, it is available to other professional organizations, and to industrial, youth, and church groups. It is managed by a full-time staff and can accommodate 150 overnight guests.

The Pinellas County Classroom Teachers Association in Florida initiated action in 1959 to develop a teachers club. The Pinellas Teachers Club now operates a country-club for its members. Facilities include a swimming pool, clubhouse, fishing lake, and picnic area.[23] Future expansion of club facilities is already being planned.

Scholarships. Scholarship assistance provided for certified teachers through professional organizations is generally limited to informational services. Some state associations gather information on scholarships available within the state and throughout the nation and supply listings of these data to their members. Others include scholarship information in their professional journals, newsletters, and other publications.

A number of state and local professional associations offer

[20] *1960–61 Handbook, The Wyoming Education Association* (Cheyenne, Wyo.: Wyoming Education Association, 1960), p. 25.

[21] *Your Association—More Than a Century of Service* (Columbia, Mo.: Missouri State Teachers Association, 1960), pp. 26–27.

[22] *MEA Handbook, op. cit.,* p. 20.

[23] *Local Color, 1959–1960* (Washington, D.C.: Department of Classroom Teachers, National Education Association, 1960), pp. 39–41.

scholarship funds to persons preparing to become teachers. In a few instances funds are granted to non-certified teachers to complete their professional preparation. Most of these scholarships are outright grants; however, some contain a proviso stipulating that the recipient must teach for a certain period after completing his training or repay the funds to the organization. Some organizations offer only loans which must be repaid within a given time interval. In 1959 the Oregon Education Association created a trust fund to establish scholarships for outstanding young men and women desiring to become teachers.[24] Scholarships of variable amounts are awarded from this fund on an annual basis with renewals possible for a total of four years. The Michigan Education Association established a similar fund in 1960.[25] A local association, the Cumberland County Classroom Teachers Association of Fayetteville, North Carolina, initiated a scholarship loan service in 1956.[26]

Travel and tour services.   For 17 years the National Education Association through its Educational Travel Division has offered teachers world-wide travel and tour opportunities. Through the services of this non-profit professional agency individual teachers and teacher groups enjoy the pleasures of efficiently planned educational travel at minimum cost. In the summer of 1962 the Division planned more than 40 educational tours for teachers.[27] These ranged in length from 18 to 54 days and included more than 66 countries. The NEA also co-sponsors many travel projects and seminars with institutions of higher learning which provide college credit for teachers. In addition to the planned travel programs it directly operates, the Educational Travel Division provides local and state associations with professional and technical assistance in planning and operating tours designed to meet personalized specifications. Many state groups including the California Teachers Association, the Wyoming Education Association, and the Colorado Education Association utilize this service in developing summer tours for their members.

[24] *Oregon Scholarships Through OEA Trust Fund, Inc.* (Portland, Ore.: Oregon Education Association, n.d.).

[25] *Procedure for Use of MEA Scholarship Fund* (Lansing, Mich.: Michigan Education Association, 1960).

[26] *Local Color, 1957–1958, op. cit.,* pp. 9–10.

[27] *Windows on the World 1962* (Washington, D.C.: Division of Educational Travel, National Education Association, 1961).

Only limited travel services are provided by local associations. Some offer occasional trips to outstanding events and places within the state or region. These are generally of one-day duration and seldom more than three days in length. A few locals sponsor trips to the annual National Education Association convention. Routes and schedules are planned to permit maximum sightseeing opportunities, and tours of this nature often range from two weeks to a month. Frequently they are co-sponsored by two or more locals or by a local and its state association.

Credit unions.   Teacher credit unions have increased considerably in recent years and have become a major development in the promotion of the economic welfare of teachers. In 1960–61 there were 1266 of these teacher agencies in operation, more than one-half of which had been organized since 1951. Total teacher membership was estimated to be in excess of 300,000. This growth and development of teacher credit unions resulted primarily from the efforts and services of national, state, and local educational associations.

A credit union is a savings and loan association owned and operated by its members. It is composed of individuals who have a common employment or interest and who agree to save together and loan to one another at low interest rates.[28] Through this co-operative pooling of resources a systematic investment program yielding good dividends can be developed, and, at the same time, the benefits of readily available low-cost loans can be assured.

All teacher credit unions are chartered either by the state or federal government. At present 44 states grant state charters and the federal law permits federal charters to be issued in all states. Therefore, interested teacher groups in 44 states may choose to be chartered either as a state or federal credit union. The provisions of both laws are usually similar; however, supervision of state chartered credit unions is provided by a state agency while federal credit unions are supervised by a federal agency.

Membership in teacher credit unions is obtained by the payment of an entrance fee (often no more than 50 cents) and the purchase of one or more shares of stock (frequently costing five dollars per

---

[28] *Credit Unions for Teachers, Discussion Pamphlet VI* (Washington, D.C.: Research Division and Department of Classroom Teachers, National Education Association, 1960), p. 1.

share). Membership in individual credit unions varies from those with less than 50 members to those with more than 10,000. The assets of individual unions range from less than $10,000 to more than $7,000,000. In addition to their basic investment and loan functions, many of these organizations offer a variety of other services. These include notary service, budget counseling, income tax service, insurance programs and protection, and check-cashing services.[29]

The actions and activities of professional associations to promote the growth and development of teacher credit unions have been continuous over a period of years. The National Education Association has maintained a Committee on Credit Unions since 1940. The purposes of this Committee are listed in the NEA Handbook as follows.

1. To keep the teaching profession continuously informed about the need for, and value of, credit unions.
2. To help the members of teacher credit unions to make efficient use of the facilities and resources available to them.
3. To make available credit union service to every school district.
4. To encourage teacher credit unions to broaden their field of membership.[30]

To accomplish their purposes the Committee periodically publishes bulletins, pamphlets, and research reports on the status of credit unions, advantages of membership, and procedures for organization. It also contributes material to the NEA Journal, organizes programs and exhibits for the annual NEA meeting, and encourages the appointment of credit union committees in state and local associations.

Almost without exception state education associations report one of their membership services to be the promotion, sponsorship, or encouragement of local and state teacher credit unions. Many have credit union committees, while others assign the responsibility of promoting credit unions to their welfare committee. State associations also publish materials on how credit unions may be established and how they function. Although each credit union is chartered as an independent agency, a number have been organized at the state

[29] *Practices and Finances of Teacher Credit Unions* (Washington, D.C.: Committee on Credit Unions, National Education Association, 1960), pp. 27–31.
[30] *NEA Handbook, op. cit.*, p. 97.

level by state teachers associations. Two of these are the Nebraska Teachers Credit Union and the Minnesota Education Association Credit Union. Membership in each is available to all members of the state education association.

The large majority of teacher credit unions have been established on the local level and in many instances local education associations have been the sponsoring agency. Local teacher associations frequently underwrite the initial organizational cost of the teachers' credit union, allocate office space and personnel, and print and mail credit union informational materials without charge.

Discount purchasing. Although many teachers have the benefit of discount purchasing, it is difficult to ascertain the scope of this service or the extent to which it is provided through the efforts of professional organizations. Many local businesses extend discount courtesies to teachers as a matter of policy and have no contact with professional organizations. In other instances discount privileges established by educational associations are disclosed only to association members. It is also known that some professional groups do not favor the service because of the public relations problems which may be involved. Yet other associations list discount purchasing as one of the financial benefits of organizational membership.

Local teacher groups more often provide discount purchasing services for their members than do state educational organizations. However, the procedures followed by local groups differ considerably. Some send their members a listing of firms offering discounts, the products or sales on which discounts apply, and the amount of the discount. Other associations maintain a telephone service which assists interested members in obtaining discount purchasing information. In some instances the local association supports or aids a separate local "discount purchasing service" which association members are entitled to join at minimum cost.

On the state level several associations circularize lists of firms which grant discounts to teachers possessing a membership card of the state organization. In contrast to this minimum service, the California Teachers Association offers its members discount purchasing opportunities through the services of the Hotel Service Bureau Buying Agency (HSB).[31] This agency obtains price quota-

31 *CTA Special Services* (Burlingame, Calif.: California Teachers Association, 1961).

tions for teachers and acts as their purchasing agent. Teachers may complete their entire transaction through the mail by sending their order and check to the HSB. However, if they prefer, they may obtain a purchase order from the HSB and make direct contact with the store or outlet which is to supply the merchandise.

Other services. Many direct welfare services are provided by local, state, and national organizations in addition to those described in the preceding pages. Although all of these are important and valuable to the teachers they assist, they are not offered by any sizable group of associations and therefore are beyond the scope of this chapter. Among this group of services, however, is one which seems worthy of identification. This is the "cash grant fund" maintained by several associations.

Labeled as a defense fund by one association, a disaster fund by another, and a personal welfare fund by a third, it typically functions as a fund from which cash grants may be made to teachers who have incurred financial crisis because of certain specified reasons. Two of these reasons are sustained illness by either a new or retired teacher to whom group insurance coverage was not available, and the unjust dismissal of a teacher from his job. Several local associations including the Portland (Maine) Teachers Association and the Casper-Midwest Classroom Teachers Association in Wyoming are known to have a fund of this nature. The Michigan Education Associaton is one state organization which has also established a fund of this type. The Association has designated it the MEA Defense Fund and has described its purpose as follows:

> Through the Defense Fund members are able to obtain sufficient finances to help overcome a crisis when regular income is not forthcoming. The purpose of the Fund is to protect members from such a crisis developing from unjust dismissal or from the violation of professional ethics by that member's superiors. Financial aid is given as an outright grant to a distressed teacher. In the event that all or part of the member's loss in salary is recovered, the difference between his total salary and the grant-in-aid may be retained by the member, and the balance is refunded to the Defense Fund.[32]

---

[32] *MEA Handbook, op. cit.,* p. 35.

CHAPTER VII

Summary

An important function of personnel administration is that of meeting the welfare needs of professional workers in school systems. These needs relate to mental and physical health, psychological viewpoints toward employment, social status in the community, and the ability to meet the economic demands of daily life.

The purposes behind welfare provisions in the personnel program are greater efficiency in carrying out the philosophy and objectives of the school system, strengthening staff cooperation, eliminating annoyances and worries which interfere with service performance, helping to bring out each individual's potential for growth and development, attracting high-grade young people into teaching, and increasing the amount of satisfaction derived from employment.

Care must be taken in formulating welfare policies and practices to provide for the non-material as well as the material needs of personnel. Both considerations have an influence on the attitudes, feelings, and efficiency of workers. It has also been discovered that the way in which policies are determined may have even more of an impact on attitudes and actions of workers than the benefits they provide.

The areas in which policies and practices should receive careful attention—aside from salary, tenure, and retirement—are health and recreation, working conditions and environment, leaves of absence, insurance protection, and benefit associations and services.

Health and Recreation

Sound health is essential for superior teaching and should be a primary interest of each school district. The concern felt by local boards of education for the physical and mental health of their teachers is reflected in the health standards established and the procedures and services they provide to enforce these standards.

The majority of states prescribe minimum physical health criteria

105

for teachers through their physical examination requirements. Frequently these criteria are considered adequate by local boards of education and they enact no supplemental physical health requirements. In contrast, other districts have detailed physical health provisions which specify some or all of the following: who must be examined; when an examination must be given; what the examination must include; who may administer the examination; and how examination records are to be processed.

Although school districts often employ medical personnel, only a limited number of districts permit these specialists to render services for teachers beyond those of a first-aid nature. Even the more common medical services provided for employees in American industry (such as consultations, examinations, and innoculations) are seldom available to teachers through the school doctor, dentist, or nurse. In a large majority of districts, however, teachers have limited health protection through provisions of state workmen's compensation laws. These laws generally offer reimbursement for medical and hospital costs and lost earnings resulting from injuries sustained in the performance of duty.

Mental health policy provisions and services for teachers are practically non-existent in local school systems. Few districts offer psychological or psychiatric counseling for teachers or have an established procedure to facilitate the referral of teachers for mental health examinations.

School districts recognize the value of recreation in the promotion of sound pupil health and provide broad pupil recreation programs, but district-sponsored recreation for teachers is uncommon. Present offerings usually consist of an infrequent cultural or social event or athletic contest. Regular school facilities, equipment, and resources could form the basis for a comprehensive teacher recreation program. From the evidence available, it appears that school systems exert only token efforts to promote community-sponsored teacher recreational events or to acquaint teachers with existing public and private recreational opportunities.

Working Conditions and Environment

It is generally recognized that teacher performance is influenced by the working conditions and environment of the school system.

Districts seeking to develop and maintain maximum staff productivity work to create a satisfying environment for teachers. Environment is regarded as the composite of district contractual provisions, administrative practices, physical surroundings, and community influences; and the districts carefully plan their actions in each of these areas. Many accept teacher participation in the formulation of policies as a valuable practice and use staff advisory committees for this purpose.

Teachers in an increasing number of districts are being informed of their contractual rights and responsibilities through the distribution of district handbooks or policy manuals. These publications include state and local rules, regulations, and procedures concerning tenure and retirement; salary schedules and methods of payment; employment periods and hours of duty; instructional and non-instructional responsibilities; grievance provisions and procedures; professional growth requirements; supplemental employment provisions; and other contractual aspects of their employment.

Greater attention is being directed to the physical characteristics of classrooms and their effect on teachers. Some districts are concerned with classroom furnishings and the environmental influence of color and design, as well as with noise and outside distractions on both teachers and pupils.

A variety of pupil grouping and placement procedures are being utilized to create a manageable task for teachers and thereby to promote pupil learning. A number of districts have policies establishing special programs for atypical children. In contrast, a large number of systems are without any written policy on class size or teacher load.

Although the range is great in the scope of services offered, the evidence seems clear that the majority of school districts recognize a responsibility to provide supervision for teachers. It is the policy of some districts to sponsor in-service growth opportunities for their teachers and to expect their participation. In other systems, teacher in-service growth is considered a personal responsibility. A number of other districts relate professional growth to salary schedules.

It seems important for districts to recognize that community influences may have a substantial effect on the working conditions and environment of teachers. Some districts reflect their concern in their policies on standards of conduct, participation in community life, and the solicitation of teachers for financial support of community activities. In general, these policies support the right of teachers to enjoy the same freedoms accorded to other citizens.

Leaves of Absence

Leaves of absence, or the right to be away from work for recognized and accepted reasons, are provided in the laws of several states and in the rules and regulations of most local school districts. Leaves of absence for sickness or injury are usually granted with pay for a specific number of days annually and the unused days may or may not be allowed to accumulate. Provisions are included in plans for reducing or preventing abuse of sick leave privileges. Sick leave may also be extended for a semester or a year in cases of serious illness or injury, but no salary is paid during the extended period.

While most boards of education make provision for maternity leave in their personnel policies, nevertheless there are a few which refuse to grant this kind of leave. The leave is generally limited to teachers who have received tenure.

Leaves for increasing the professional knowledge and skill of teachers are recognized widely. They include sabbatical leave for a semester or a year; extended leave for a semester or a year; leave for attendance at conferences, conventions, clinics, and workshops; leave for visits to other schools; exchange teaching, both domestic and foreign; and services in professional organizations.

In addition, school districts permit leave for illness at home where the presence of the teacher is needed; leave for death in the immediate family; leave for the observance of religious holidays; leave for answering court summons and for serving on juries; leave for military duty; leave for attendance at an examination for a university degree; leave for attendance at the graduation exercises of a son or daughter; paternity leave for the expected birth of a child; leave for quarantine of a house in which the teacher lives; leave for service in a local or state legislative body; and leave for a wedding in the immediate family.

SUMMARY

Insurance Protection

Another important aspect of staff welfare is group insurance and the protection it affords against unforseen emergencies that may cut deeply into the health and economic security of the teacher and his dependents. Issued to a number of persons, as a group, who are employed by a company or an institution or who are members of an organization, it can be purchased at lower rates than individual policies. No medical examination is required, and age limits are seldom established for eligibility. It may be converted into individual insurance at the termination of employment or membership at higher premium rates.

Group life insurance is issued as a one-year, renewable policy. The amount that can be purchased seldom exceeds two to three thousand dollars except where the policy is taken out by a teachers' association for its members. The premium rate is usually paid by the teacher although boards of education in some districts carry all or part of the cost.

Group accident and health insurance, often called accident and disability insurance, replaces in part the income lost during sustained periods of disability from accident or illness and provides a lump sum for death or dismemberment.

Group hospital insurance provides against expenses incurred in hospital confinement, with benefits varying according to the policy. As a supplement, teachers may enroll in a medical-surgical plan to cover a broader range of expenses for themselves and their families. Even greater protection may be procured through group major medical insurance. This insurance covers bills when expenses exceed a fixed amount over and above the benefits received from the basic hospital-medical-surgical plan.

Group income protection insurance, also issued as group health insurance, provides the teacher with a steady source of income during periods of disability from illness or accident, and especially after accumulated sick leave allowance has been exhausted. A principal sum is paid for loss of life by accident or for loss of specified parts of the body.

Finally, group liability insurance may be bought by the teacher against economic loss resulting from civil law suits in which damages are awarded against him.

Benefit Associations and Services

Professional educational associations are concerned with the procurement of welfare benefits for teachers. These volunteer groups exist on the local, state, and national level to improve the services rendered by the profession and also to improve the economic, social, and professional welfare of their members. The largest of these organizations is the National Education Association. Through the work of its departments and committees, its affiliate associations in each state, and approximately 7000 local associations throughout the nation, numerous welfare benefits are made available to teachers.

In addition to the psychological and financial benefits which accrue to teachers from the work of professional organizations with boards of education, legislative bodies, and the general public, these associations offer many direct services to their members. Among those commonly provided are medical services, including blood banks; endowed hospital rooms, and group insurance; legal assistance; credit union sponsorship; discount purchasing plans; community orientation activities; and guidance services, including research and preparation of technical information, surveys, and investigations.

Other services less frequently offered, but of a highly beneficial nature include cooperative housing facilities for senior and retired teachers; non-profit travel and tour programs for individual teachers and teacher groups; scholarship information and loan funds; professional placement service at minimum cost; and recreational programs and facilities including clubs, lodges, swimming and fishing sites, and camp installations.

Bibliography

Brook, George C., *Summary Report of Teacher Fringe Benefits in Large Public School Systems: Populations of 200,000 or More.* Chicago, Illinois: Bureau of Research and Statistics, Chicago Public Schools, May, 1958.

Caplow, Theodore, *The Sociology of Work.* Minneapolis, Minnesota: University of Minnesota Press, 1954.

Castetter, William B., *Administering the School Personnel Program,* Chapter 12. New York: The Macmillan Company, 1962.

Chamberlain, Leo M. and Leslie W. Kindred, *The Teacher and School Organization,* Chapter 22, 3rd ed. Englewood Cliffs, New Jersey: Prentice-Hall, Inc., 1958.

Chruden, Herbert J. and Arthur W. Sherman, Jr., *Personnel Management,* Chapters 12, 15, 17, 26. Cincinnati, Ohio: South-Western Publishing Company, 1959.

Company Medical and Health Programs, Studies in Personnel Policy No. 171. New York: National Industrial Conference Board, Inc., 1959.

Conditions of Work for Quality Teaching, Department of Classroom Teachers. Washington, D.C.: National Education Association, 1960.

Edwards, Newton, *The Courts and the Public Schools,* rev. ed. Chicago, Illinois: The University of Chicago Press, 1955.

Gauerke, Warren E., *Legal and Ethical Responsibilities of School Personnel.* Englewood Cliffs, New Jersey: Prentice-Hall, Inc., 1959.

Glenn, J. E., "Military Leaves Law Provisions Described for Teachers' Use," *New York State Education,* 47 (May, 1960), 42.

Johns, E. B., "Your Health Insurance Program," *NEA Journal,* 49 (September, 1960), 88.

Jucius, Michael J., *Personnel Management,* Chapters 16, 23, 26, 27, 29. Homewood, Illinois: Richard D. Irwin, Inc., 1959.

Lewis, A. C., "Health Insurance for Teachers," *New York State Education,* 46 (October, 1958), 44.

Lieberman, Myron, *Education as a Profession,* Chapters 9, 10. Englewood Cliffs, New Jersey: Prentice-Hall, Inc., 1956.

Little, E., "How Much Sick Leave is Enough?," *Texas Outlook,* 44 (April, 1960), 33–35.

Nigro, Felix A., *Public Personnel Administration,* Chapters 10, 12. New York: Holt, Rinehart & Winston, Inc., 1959.

Putnam, Rufus A., *Preliminary Report on Fringe Benefits Questionnaire.* Minneapolis, Minnesota: Minneapolis Public Schools, 1957.

111

Remmlein, Madeline K., *School Law,* Chapters 8, 9, 12, 2nd ed. Danville, Illinois: Interstate Printers and Publishers, Inc., 1962.

Roethlisberger, F. J., *Management and Morale.* Cambridge, Massachusetts: Harvard University Press, 1949.

Staff Relations in School Administration, 33rd Yearbook, American Association of School Administrators. Washington, D.C.: National Education Association, 1955.

Survey of Employee Benefits in 83 Southern California School Districts. Los Angeles, California: Cooperative Personnel Services, California State Personnel Board, 1959.

Survey of Fringe Benefits for Regular Teachers. Los Angeles, California: Personnel Division, Los Angeles Public Schools, April, 1958.

The Status of the American Public-School Teacher, Research Bulletin, Vol. 35, No. 1. Washington, D.C.: Research Division, National Education Association, 1957.

Waterman, B., "Health Insurance Benefits for Teachers: A Progress Report," *New York State Education,* 48 (April, 1961), 33.

Index

A

Abington, Pennsylvania, 33, 36, 61, 69
Accident and health insurance, 80-81
Allentown, Pennsylvania, 33
Altman, Emil, 21
Altoona, Pennsylvania, 53
American Association for Health, Physical Education, and Recreation, 22
Arlington, Virginia, 33, 54

B

Beaver Falls, Pennsylvania, 48
Birmingham Classroom Teachers Association, Alabama, 98
Brook, George C., 111
Brookline, Massachusetts, 88

C

Cafeterias, 47
California Teachers Association, 96, 100, 103
Caplow, Theodore, 111
Cash grant fund, 104
Casper-Midwest Classroom Teachers Association, Wyoming, 104
Castetter, William B., 111
Centennial Joint Schools, Pennsylvania, 51
Chamberlain, Leo M., 111
Cheltenham, Pennsylvania, 37
Chruden, Herbert J., 111
Clark County School District, Clark County, Nevada, 37
Classrooms, 46
Class size, 50-51
Colorado Education Association, 100
Community recreation, 27-28
Contracts, teachers, 29-30
Cooperative Personnel Services, 112
Counseling and placement services of educational associations, 95-97
Court summons, 71-72
Credit unions, 101-103
Cumberland County Classroom Teachers Association of Fayetteville, North Carolina, 100

D

Death in family, 70-71
Delaware State Education Association, 95
Denver, Colorado, 17, 24
Des Moines Educational Association, 81
Detroit, Michigan, 44, 87
Discount purchasing, 103-104
District No. 3, Boulder County, Colorado, 36
District of Columbia, 33, 59, 65

E

Eau Clair, Wisconsin, 88
Education associations:
  achievements, 91-92
  benefits for teachers, 91-92
  cash grant fund, 104
  counseling and placement services, 95-97
  credit unions, 101-103
  discount purchasing, 103-104
  housing services, 97-98
  legal services, 94-95
  medical services, 93-94
  National Education Association, 90
  recreational facilities, 98-99
  scholarships, 99-100
  special purposes, 89
  teacher needs, 91
  travel and tour services, 100-101
  welfare benefits, 110
Educational Research Service, 32
Edwards, Newton, 111
El Paso, Texas, 60, 61, 64, 88
El Paso County, Colorado, 25
Exchange teaching, 68
Extended leave, 67
Extra pay, 32

F

Fargo, North Dakota, 13
Federal Housing Authority, 98
Fort Wayne, Indiana, 51
Fulbright Act, 68

113